FIT *2* FINISH

Praise for

FIT *2* FINISH

"I would encourage coaches of all ages to read this book. Wendy LeBolt is a pioneer in the game of soccer, and this book brings out the best of her teaching and development methodology. As the landscape of soccer and all youth sports continues to change and evolve, you will find *Fit2Finish* full of practical information that creates energy while you read it. Wendy's passion, expertise, and real-life lessons in the field of player and team development will keep you intrigued from start to finish. Do yourself, your players and your team a favor and follow her advice; you will be glad you did!"

—Larry R. Best
BRYC 95 Elite, BRYC Elite Director of Coaching—Girls

"With today's youth athlete facing the rigorous physical demands of the modern game, best practices for sports performance are more critical than ever. Wendy LeBolt's invaluable compendium of information in *Fit2Finish* provides the perfect balance of practical wisdom and professional advice and is a must-read for anyone committed to youth development."

—Michael Calabretta
Wake Forest Women's Soccer

"Wendy LeBolt's book *Fit2Finish* takes the reader on an informative journey through the complex issues that face young athletes. She has combined her experiences as a coach and sport science professional into a book full of information for anyone seeking to develop those in their sport care. Coaches, athletes and parents will enjoy this book, as it combines scientific information with practical application."

—Paul Shaw
Coaching Education Director
Virginia Youth Soccer Association

"I've experienced firsthand how Dr. LeBolt has guided kids to enhance their athletic performance, to be healthier and more fit athletes and to reduce the risk of injuries. All of this is accomplished by educating them on topics such as flexibility, strengthening, balance, coordination, proper warm-up, stretching, cool down, recovery and nutrition. Her passion and genuine care for the kids lays the foundation for the insightful, powerful, effective, purposeful, influential and, most importantly, *fun* training provided by *Fit2Finish*."

—Gerardo Ramirez
Vienna Youth Soccer Director of Coaching
Virginia Youth Soccer Association District Staff Coach

"Wendy started working with my team when they were very young; she introduced the program to us and stayed with us through many years. In the early years, when the kids were young, it was serious teaching brought to the kids in the form of fun and games, an approach that really worked well. As they became older and more mature, the instruction always evolved with them and was captivating each time.

"Over 9 years of working with Wendy, we only had one knee injury, and that was to a recent addition to the team who hadn't had the benefit of Wendy's training for very long. As anyone who has spent much time with highly competitive women's soccer sadly knows, knee injuries, particularly non-contact injuries, are a common element of the sport, and it's almost unheard of to have a team go 9 years without a serious knee injury. I highly recommend Wendy's program; I'm sure you'll benefit from it as much as we did."

—Rich Gleason

Women's Youth Soccer Coach

Repeat Virginia State Champions

4-year National League Member

"*Fit2Finish* is a wealth of great information for parents, players and coaches. The book provides answers and insight to fitness questions youth coaches encounter on a regular basis. Wendy uses modern day training solutions with a common sense approach. This handbook is a must read for serious youth soccer coaches!"

—Mike Jorden

Technical Director, Chantilly Soccer Club

Past coach of two Region I Championship teams,

two Region I finalists, and ten Virginia State Cup Champions

"Dr. LeBolt's experience as a parent and coach, combined with her expertise as a scientist, brings thousands of hours of observation, evaluation and research to the forefront in an easy-to-use resource guide for coaches. *Fit2Finish* provides insight for practitioners at all levels in the quest to make athletes as fit as possible with scientifically based programs that address the issues of anaerobic and aerobic energy systems, requirements and training; neuromuscular pathways; fitness prescription;

identifying weakness; overload principle; overtraining; return-to-play; stretching, flexibility and recovery; periodization; and nutrition.

"If a coach commits to being their best, being equipped with the science to back up their training is critical. *Fit2Finish* provides the information in a succinct and practical manner. You don't need to be a scientist, but you can use this book as a pocket guide to better understand your athletes' anatomy and physiology, the background of soccer kinesiology and the drills/training that you can use to maximize their performance in a safe way.

"*Fit2Finish* provides sound practices in the science of fitness while giving coaches simple ways to incorporate these into their own training programs. Dr. LeBolt lays out a plan for coaches of both boys and girls, at all levels, in order to improve fitness in a safe manner. Most importantly, she does so without increasing the time demands on the coaches or the athletes."

—**Tanya Vogel**

Senior Associate Athletic Director, Northern Arizona University
Former head coach, George Washington University Women's Soccer
First women's soccer player inducted into the GWU Hall of Fame

"Kudos to Dr. LeBolt for such fantastic work on a subject that is so vitally important for coaches (in particular, youth coaches) to facilitate coaching education and knowledge. I can say with firm resolve that Dr. LeBolt's approach to fitness, training and developing a method which places athletes first is must-read material. Coaches at every level should put this book at the top of their list and keep it close by as a constant reference guide."

—**Jim Nieves**

Youth, high school and collegiate-level coach for over 20 years

"Technical stuff to be sure, but if you've had a child go through injury, or coached several young players who have, this advice will be invaluable! Nothing is more difficult than to watch your player go down to an injury—even worse if it is your own child. Nothing is better than to see them recover from that injury to be able to take part again in the sports and the games they love so much!

"Keeping your young athletes in the game mentally is always a challenge, and keeping them physically fit and able to compete when faced with such demanding schedules is also becoming tougher and tougher. Dr. LeBolt's methods and training will help keep them fit and prepared—the rest is up to you!"

—Fred Matthes
Executive in professional soccer and basketball for over 25 years
Parent and long-time youth soccer coach
Former collegiate-level soccer player (UCLA)

"I believe that most elite-level coaches overtrain their athletes and that, in the end, their training programs do as much harm as good. Elite-level coaches and athletes alike would do well to read this book and to implement this realistic and effective approach."

—Tom Larrick
Youth soccer coach and parent of a Division I collegiate athlete

"Wendy's tremendous understanding of the human body and compassion for young athletes makes this a must-have practical guide for youth coaches."

—Lisa Bishop
Former collegiate soccer player and youth soccer coach for 13 years

"I want my daughter to be a life-long athlete, not just to be able to play at a high level until she gets injured. Dr. LeBolt's expertise and advice show how to make this possible, and I am very grateful!"

—Laurie Phillips

Long-time soccer parent,
former collegiate athlete and current competitor

FIT 2 FINISH

Keeping Your Soccer Players in the Game

Wendy LeBolt, PhD

NEW YORK

FIT 2 FINISH
Keeping Your Soccer Players in the Game

Published in New York, New York, by Morgan James Publishing. Morgan James and The Entrepreneurial Publisher are trademarks of Morgan James, LLC. www.MorganJamesPublishing.com

The Morgan James Speakers Group can bring authors to your live event. For more information or to book an event visit The Morgan James Speakers Group at www.TheMorganJamesSpeakersGroup.com.

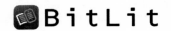

A FREE eBook edition is available
with the purchase of this print book

CLEARLY PRINT YOUR NAME IN THE BOX ABOVE

Instructions to claim your free eBook edition:
1. Download the BitLit app for Android or iOS
2. Write your name in UPPER CASE in the box
3. Use the BitLit app to submit a photo
4. Download your eBook to any device

ISBN 978-1-63047-214-6 paperback
ISBN 978-1-63047-215-3 eBook
ISBN 978-1-63047-216-0 hardcover
Library of Congress Control Number:
2014937576

Cover Design by:
Chris Treccani
www.3dogdesign.net

Interior Design by:
Bonnie Bushman
bonnie@caboodlegraphics.com

In an effort to support local communities, raise awareness and funds, Morgan James Publishing donates a percentage of all book sales for the life of each book to Habitat for Humanity Peninsula and Greater Williamsburg.

Get involved today, visit
www.MorganJamesBuilds.com.

Habitat
for Humanity®
Peninsula and
Greater Williamsburg
Building Partner

In memory of Donald C. Paup, PhD:
teacher, mentor, friend, coach and
champion in sport and in life

Table of Contents

Foreword

Dr. Wendy LeBolt and I first teamed up almost 15 years ago when I was the coach of her daughter's U9 team. Fast forward about 6 years, and we were working side by side with a couple of my youth club teams. She brought ACL prevention training that I knew those girls needed. Dr. LeBolt also kept a close eye on the George Mason University team where I have been head coach since 2004. Observing training and talking with my staff landed us in deep conversations about the health of prospective players and injuries that were overtaking them. She queried me about the college game; I asked her about the youth game—because now I had a U9 of my own who loved the game. Like every parent, I wanted to keep her healthy. Like every coach, I wanted to help her succeed. Injuries were the one thing she needed to avoid, and Dr. LeBolt knew about preventing injuries.

Injuries in youth sports are growing at a frenetic pace, and they are impacting players who come to me at the college level.

Not just ACL injuries, but major overuse injuries. Fully one third to one half of my incoming freshman class—Division I players who are among the best in the country—is injured when they arrive at GMU. Most are overuse problems that need to be addressed; improper training and preparation at the youth level have landed them there.

Dr. LeBolt nails the cause in *Fit2Finish*: the game alone doesn't provide the proper environment for healthy training adaptation. But many youth coaches lack the proper knowledge to train the youth soccer player. My time on the sidelines of youth games has made this very plain. Add to this the trend in the environment of youth soccer in this country—funded from the bottom up, not the top down, so you have to pay to play—which leaves coaches feeling scrutinized by the parents paying. I constantly hear coaches criticized for doing overall fitness training that may appear non-soccer-related. Expectations are for more games and more playing time. More training, more coaching, more games and more stress leads almost inevitably to more injuries. We are overdoing it! Are we surprised? This is America, home of the supersized McDonald's fries!

As coaches of elite players, we operate under the SAID (Specific Adaptations to Imposed Demands) principle—meaning activities should replicate the *demands* of the game, and training design requires gradually adapting to these demands. Supersizing does not make them better or faster at the elite level, and certainly not at the youth level. Development takes time and special care when the bodies we are training are still growing. *Fit2Finish* translates the SAID principles for the youth game and the youth coach. Dr. LeBolt spells out the importance of proper training using activities designed to develop overall fitness, while keeping in mind developmental needs. Plus, she makes them fun.

She zeroes in on three negative effects of the current "train only with the game" approach: sidedness, patterns/habits and repetition. Sidedness, players defaulting to favor their strong side under pressure, is human nature. This makes the weakness even weaker and invites injury. Patterns of habitual movement require compensation, which leads to imbalance and often injury. Finally, repetition of "what works," while it may bring short-term success, opens the door to perpetuating the imbalances. Perpetually calling on the acting muscles overtrains them at the expense of the stabilizing and supporting muscles. This repetitive use without proper recovery can be a source of imbalance and excessive fatigue, especially in growing athletes, and ultimately a cause of injury. This is not a good long-term strategy. And we want these kids to keep playing strong. I sure do; I want 'em in my program! Balanced training with proper recovery is key. Dr. LeBolt steps you through the process of developing this with your kids and your players on your training fields.

Fit2Finish will serve as a bible to many parents of budding young stars. As a soccer (fútbol) mom, an American football mom, a club coach and a head college coach, I wear many hats. I see where youth sports training is getting derailed. Dr. LeBolt gets us back on track. Your child looks to you as a parent and/or coach to get a strong, healthy start. The fact that you are reading this book shows that you care about doing this right. Invite Dr. LeBolt to show you how to watch your athletes move, recognize deficiencies and train them back into balance and strong performance. This is a resource you will come back to again and again as they grow up in the game. It's a user's manual for youth coaching at every level. I plan to keep a copy handy.

—Diane Drake
Head Women's Soccer Coach, George Mason University

Introduction:
Fit for the Game

When I was growing up playing sports, nobody ever got hurt, at least not seriously. I don't remember a single teammate ever complaining of knee pain, shin pain, heel pain or hip pain. Today nearly all young athletes eventually experience at least one of these maladies. What has changed since the "good ole days?"

Plenty. For starters, more are kids playing. More than 44 million American children play competitive youth sports, according to a 2008 survey done by the National Council on Youth Sports. Girls' participation continues to rise but still is somewhat less than boys'. There are more sports, more games and more competitions all year round. Sometimes multiple sports overlap in the same season. We're starting children younger and younger, placing them on teams coached by well-meaning volunteers, usually parents, who may not recognize how entrenched they are in a culture that celebrates—often worships—the champion.

Today is all about the "more." We want to give our kids more of what used to be so good for us. And so we have. But it hasn't always been so good for them.

Yes, we want them to be active and healthy. Soccer seems the perfect game for this, and we can start them young. But youth soccer today demands a great deal, especially as they move up through the competitive ranks. Simply for their survival they need to be fit.

Do you think your young soccer players can become fit for the game just by playing it? It makes sense in a way. Certainly the game puts all the right demands on them. It's the most specific training they can get, right? They run and jump and stop and start and pass and kick and shoot and tackle. The game has all of these. Doing them must be the way to train them. Right?

I used to think so until I began attending my kids' games and then started coaching them. That's when I saw kids limping, hobbling and on crutches. Some wore braces to protect their surgically repaired joints or to keep from having surgery. At first I thought these kids' injuries were isolated events or just their bad luck, but soon I learned that this was widespread, affecting what seemed like legions of kids. Injury rates were on a steep climb. Some injuries, like anterior cruciate ligament injuries in girls, were even being called epidemic.

Parents from those teams, who knew my training and teaching background in health, fitness and sports medicine, begged me to address these issues for the sake of their kids. I had three young soccer players of my own, so I understood the issues and concerns both as a parent and as a coach.

Sports are still good for our kids. Or they can be. But unfortunately there is no going back to the old days. Sports done well offer physical, mental, psychological and emotional benefits to our kids in a real-life, low-risk, right-sized setting. So, if it's so good for them, how come they are getting hurt? Dropping out? Or stuck on the sidelines?

Risks come with taking the field. This has always been true. But I believe the benefits far outweigh the risks. They did for me. I now see how formative my youth sports experiences were. The playing field is where I tried on life to see what fit and what didn't. The value of sport is way too important for our kids to lose out on.

I wanted them to play, and play healthy, but how? I waded into the environment of youth sports today with a divining rod and asked:

- Why are so many kids getting injured?
- Why are so many kids dropping out?
- How can we get and keep all the kids playing?
- What can we do to keep the kids playing who want to play hard?
- How can we prepare kids for what the game today asks of them?

This handbook is the result of asking those questions. The examples I use are from my experience working with soccer athletes of all ages and at a variety of playing levels. They come from the ranks of rec leagues, club teams, elite teams and college play. The need for a foundation of healthy fitness is the same for each because their bodies are what's in play and at stake.

I do not set out here to right the culture of youth sports. Many voices are speaking on that subject and participating in that conversation with a lot of energy. (See Resources section for a reading list on this topic.) I am, rather, on a rescue mission. We must address the "too much, too early, at too high a price." While we go about changing the culture, the kids who are currently in it need saving. And so do those who will come after them.

We need to do the following:

- Prepare kids physically for the appropriate level of play
- Balance the demands on kids to allow their bodies to strengthen and grow
- Do this within the time kids have apportioned in their often over-committed days

And by the way, I refuse to lose the fun. Why? Because without the fun, they won't want to do it, and they certainly won't keep doing it. And that's my ultimate goal as a fitness professional, trainer and coach, but especially as a parent: to help kids develop bodies they will use well their whole lives, not just because it's good for them but because they want to. Our bodies were loaned to us for just one lifetime; we need to treat them that way.

In the chapters that follow, we will:

- Address the demands of the game on your players
- Identify weaknesses and imbalances that make them injury-prone

- Look at the basic anatomy and physiology that create movement
- Design a physical training plan appropriate for your players
- Learn to implement training within your current practice setting (see video links in Fitness Games chart, chapter 4, and in Resources section)
- Incorporate rest and nutrition for growth, performance and recovery
- Address possible injuries and the means to facilitate safe return to play
- Adopt fitness and injury prevention as a strategy for success

I guess you could call this a "survival" strategy. Survival of the fittest, with a twist. As Darwin defined it, "Fitness is the ability to survive, reproduce and adapt in a specific environment." Sound applicable to today's youth sports environment? In fitness we use the "SAID" principle: Specific Adaptations to Imposed Demands. There's just one catch: the game alone doesn't provide the proper environment for healthy adaptation. But as coaches and parents we can help our players grow and develop (adapt) by applying training (reproduce) in a way that goes beyond survival. It will sustain them. Now, that's fitness.

This handbook will show you how to plug effective and fun fitness into your practices, preparing players for stronger play with fewer injuries. These kids will leave it all on the field because they want to, not because you told them to. That'll make them winners whenever the final whistle blows.

Kids and Fitness:
What Does the Game Require?

Most coaches know the skills of the game. They study tactics and strategies and provide drills and set-ups to teach them. But most coaches have little or no formal training in "fitness for sport." Generally, they regard game fitness as being able to run the fastest for the longest, something we can see and measure. And running is undoubtedly part of being fit for the game, especially for advanced players who may cover 5 to 8 miles in stop-and-start traffic. But fitness for the game of soccer requires a lot more than just running.

The list of physical skills required of a soccer player is a long one: walking, running, cruising, jogging, sprinting, heading, jumping, landing, starting, stopping, cutting, turning, tackling, passing, shooting, sliding, shuffling sideways, accelerating, decelerating, dropping backwards, and more. Then we add the ball and insist that players are fast and accurate for up to 90 minutes. The point is this: the demands of the game are complex. You couldn't possibly teach it all. The game must do that.

But fitness for these basic movements requires training that we may not see or measure directly. Athletes need muscular strength, neuromuscular coordination and flexibility at each of the joints called into action. Add to this the need for endurance, speed, agility and power, all of which require functional whole body training for performance. You could have the kids in the gym all morning and on the track all afternoon, but there's a better way when it comes to youth sports. Incorporate fitness into functional, sport-specific training that addresses the demands of the game and targets the needs of your players.

This handbook will show you how to do just that. We'll start with the game and the movements and skills required to play it. Where movement falters and a correction is needed, we'll address the underlying shortcoming, decide what needs strengthening, stretching or balance and then design an appropriate exercise. But we won't stop there. That exercise will be folded into a game, skill or drill that requires little or no equipment so you can take it straight to the field. You'll be problem solving with your athletes based on a solid foundation of information in the field of exercise science, but they'll think they're just having fun.

Why can't players get their fitness just from playing the game?
The game is a great teacher, and the "just the game" approach has been taught by soccer educators for quite some time. But

when it comes to fitness, the "just playing" is hobbling today's players by introducing:

- Sidedness: They tend to favor their strong side because under pressure they default to their strength. That makes weaknesses even weaker.
- Patterns and Repetition: They favor certain muscles and learned movement patterns (e.g., inner thigh for passing). This accentuates the acting muscles but disregards the stabilizing and support muscles needed to provide balance to execute the skill.
- Habits: They engage in habitual movement patterns that may be disadvantageous from an injury standpoint (e.g., to stop and turn, girls tend to stay more upright, causing quadriceps to overpower weaker hamstrings and put knee ligaments at risk).
- Overtraining: They subject muscles to repetitive use without proper recovery. This can be a source of imbalance and excessive fatigue, especially in growing athletes, and ultimately a cause of injury (e.g., running and knee extension in kicking activities pull on the patellar tendon again and again, often resulting in knee soreness and pain).

There is some good news about the "just the game" approach. It gives our children the chance to run and play and use their bodies, something they may not do as regularly as we did in the "good ole days." The body, when well used, teaches itself how to balance and move, given the chance. This is easy to spot in the active, athletic kid. It's very different from movements that are "taught" step by step—those that look learned rather than natural. The most effective strategy is to help the kids make movement natural.

I don't propose breaking down each of these movements into the muscles engaged and the order in which they're activated to accomplish the perfect strike. We'll leave that to the biomechanics specialists. That sounds more like the adult approach to working out in the weight room: isolate the muscle groups and train them one by one as you work your way down the circuit. Fun? Nah. Not for kids with play in mind.

How do we use the game to plan the fitness?

Watch your players to see how they move. Is it smooth? Are they balanced? Do they fall or get shoved off the ball? Are they favoring one side, one leg, one direction or one movement? Are players tired early? Breathing hard? Losing ground to teammates or opponents? Which players are getting winded and when? Does all this sound hard? Not really. What you're looking for is individually smooth movement resulting in flowing team play. Think Michael Jordan, poetry in motion. You know it when you see it, and you know it when it's disrupted. You must become a movement pattern observer, seeing both the big picture and the individual components.

In the next chapter we'll look at some basics of the anatomy and physiology of movement, consider what moves and how it moves and focus on the stuff every coach needs to know. I'll share some diagnostic activities and assessments that you can perform with your players to identify where their weaknesses and imbalances are.

Then you'll know where to focus their training or how to adjust their playing environment to bring them up to speed. Once corrected, their play will become more fluid because their whole bodies will be engaged. Not only will you see it, they'll feel it. And that will make them more powerful, confident athletes.

Your job will be to design activities into your practices that address the weaknesses, most commonly sidedness, patterns, unhealthy habits and overuse. Basically, you'll be using the game to see what it's not providing your players, then adding back healthy fitness to recover balance and fluid movement.

Chapter 3 walks you through the design and progression of fitness for your players. Chapter 4 addresses common issues with suggested activities for different age groups. Chapter 5 provides information and detailed application of probably the most under-used weapons in the coach's fitness arsenal: rest and recovery. Chapter 6 addresses fueling your athletes and includes take-home sheets and quizzes for your players and their families.

Chapter 7 tackles the injury issue. Injuries are part of the game, whether we like it or not. Proper fitness will help to minimize injuries to your players, but not all injuries are preventable. Included in Appendix F is a 'cheat sheet' of common injuries and their symptoms, and recommendations for managing recovery and return to play.

Before we really dig in, here are some basic guidelines I've discovered while working with teams of boys and girls of all ages.

1. Consider the developmental age in addition to chronological age when designing or adopting prescribed fitness activities with your team, especially if they represent a range of abilities. Fitness drills are designed to challenge, and they can injure an athlete if he or she cannot or does not perform them correctly. This can be due to a lack of strength or a lack of coordination. Or they may just be horsing around. Don't insist kids perform a drill if they cannot do it properly.

   • If they lack body control or coordination, back off to a simpler drill, slow it down and/or lower expectations.

   • If they demonstrate weakness, which usually takes the form of an imbalance such as a "rolling inward" of the knee, falling to one side or inability to maintain form throughout the whole exercise, identify the weak muscles and challenge them specifically, insisting on proper form.

   • If they're horsing around, then…

2. Know what your players are capable of physically, mentally, socially and emotionally. Whether they realize it or not, coaches often tend to coach kids in the way they would teach adults. They explain (several times) and demonstrate (sometimes with little accuracy) and then correct every step of the way. Kids rarely do well with this approach because their attention spans are short and they came to play.

So before we launch into the training plan, let's look at the physical and emotional nature of girls and boys at various ages. Here are some general characterizations[1] and a brief assessment of the "gender gap" which, whether it's due to nurture or nature, we know exists. Awareness of these differences will assist the coach in reaching and connecting with children, whatever their age.

Beginners

- 6–8-year-olds: easily distracted, egocentric, tend to cluster, easily fatigued, love movement, need clear directions. They process one task at a time.
- 8–10-year-olds: team identity is beginning; more focus on drills and ball control. They know "who is good." Challenge them to work on their own. They need concise, purposeful instructions.
- 10–12-year-olds: tend to compare with others, can focus on a team objective, like to work at improving.

Intermediate/Juniors

- 12–14-year-olds: read the game, assertiveness, growth spurts. They are at risk of growth plate injuries, and are subject to "growing pains," which generally are over-use injuries in kids who are active.
- 14–16-year-olds: apathy, stubbornness, moodiness; for boys winning is most important, less so for girls. They

---

1   Adapted from Raymond Verheijen, *Conditioning for Soccer* (Spring City, PA: Reedswain Videos and Books, 1998).

are learning to use their individual skills within the team framework.
- 16–18-year-olds: more mentally and physically stable. They want to be challenged to improve.

The gender gap

Taken as broad gender populations, there are no genetic differences in playing abilities. Nonetheless:

- Boys are more often brought up handling a ball, while girls must develop "feeling" for the ball.
- Boys focus on their own performance, while girls try to achieve through a cooperative effort.
- Through middle school ages, boys and girls can benefit from playing together. Boys learn a more team-centric, cooperative approach, and girls tend to play more purposefully.
- Girls reach puberty somewhat earlier than boys, so between 12 and 14 they are more developed physically and more mature mentally. By 15, boys catch up physically; by 18, mentally. Thus gender-mixed play in high school favors the superior strength, speed and power of boys. Except for the most advanced, superior female players, uni-gender play is advised.
- If you've coached both, you can add your own distinctions. Good coaching demands this.

Attention, girls' coaches: one of the reasons for caution as your female players get older is the increased risk of injury, relative to boys, that we have seen in the last two decades. Anterior cruciate ligament tears and meniscal injuries are 5 or 6 times higher in girls than in boys. Also, concussions, currently being called an epidemic in youth sports, are a larger risk for girls than boys. Speed and force of play may be a culprit, mixed with body mechanics and anatomic and neuromuscular differences. Coaches of girls should be well versed in gender-specific training for their population of players. Head to chapter 7 immediately if you can't wait.

What is fitness for, anyway?

Fitness is what allows you to play your very best and to execute skills and strategy as effectively in the last minutes as you did in the first. Fitness is essential, but most kids don't like "conditioning days" because the fun is in the game. Somehow we have made fitness into work and have lost the fun. Challenge, development, races and friendly competition are fitness at its best—through them, your players work hard and push each other to improve. This doesn't need to be grueling; frankly, you'll get more out of them if they enjoy what they are doing, or at least see the purpose in doing it.

Please hear me in this one preaching moment: NEVER use fitness as a punishment. Not if they play poorly, not if they misbehave, not as a penalty for losing and especially not if you're angry. This kind of fitness has no place in youth sports. It discourages kids from exercise and may cause kids to drop out of sports altogether.

Please use the tools provided in this handbook to identify physical shortcomings and plan training and recovery activities.

Then put them into a game, an activity or a sport-specific drill for your players. You might even think of it as tricking them into playing in a way that is healthy. Just don't let them know it's good for them, and they'll do it happily. Chapter 4 will give you lots of examples, but the fun is in identifying what works for your own players. Or empower the kids and let them come up with ideas themselves. That'll launch all the power they'll need to head straight for the finish.

2

Sport Anatomy and Physiology:
What Makes the Body Work?

Do you know a performance kid when you see one? How about a performance automobile? How do you tell? By how they're built and how they move.

Whether you know it or not, you're an amateur anatomist and physiologist, and a mechanic to boot. To start us off, we'll take a look at the young athlete's body as a performance machine.

- The parts
- How they're put together
- How they move
- The engine, timing and lubrication

Consider this a sort of owner's manual for the kids on your lot. You need to know the basics to help them hit the accelerator, navigate the turns and brake when necessary. Whether your team consists of Ferraris or Fiats, your goal is the same: reliable, high-quality performance from each kid on the lot.

Now, each young body comes with its own monkey wrench. They're growing. And areas of new growth are as fragile as they are critical, so we'll look at anatomy and physiology with an eye on the growing body. Of course, any machine requires proper care and maintenance, and we'll get there in chapters 5 and 6. Repairs are often unavoidable, so we'll visit that in chapter 7.

For now, let's take a look at what kids' bodies are made of: bones, joints, connective tissues, muscles, nerves and the heart. If you really hated this subject in school, no worries. I understand. I taught it to hundreds of college students, many of whom didn't want to be there at first. Most of them soon discovered that learning about the body was pretty cool and quite useful. I trust you will, too.

Bones

Bones are alive. Most people are surprised to hear this. They picture a hanging Halloween skeleton or an ancestor unearthed at an anthropological dig. Our skeletons form the basic framework of our bodies, but each bone is an active organ made up of an intricate arrangement of fibers, cells and spaces, complete with blood vessels that supply nutrients and remove waste from cells that lay down new bone and take away the old. This is how growth, repair and remodeling take place. This happens your whole life long, but it's particularly pronounced in kids.

Long bones, true to their name, form the structure of the length of the limbs. These consist of a shaft with oddly shaped bumps and indentations at each end. These ends are shaped to fit together with the "next" bone in the skeleton chain to form a joint, or articulation. This "fit" is not an accident. The pushing or pulling on bones stimulates bone cells to respond. Thus, they are shaped according to their stresses. This allows bones to adapt to their environment, and it's why "weight-bearing" exercise is so important to bone health. Even in adults, after bones have achieved their maximum length, changes in circumference and density of the long bones continue.

Kids' bones, of course, are doing more than remodeling. They are also lengthening, resulting in their entire skeleton changing rapidly. Bones grow longer in two places: at the center and on

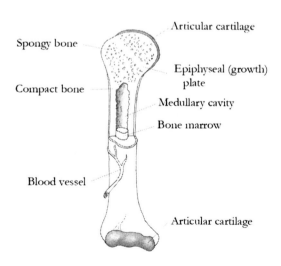

Figure 1. Long bone sectioned to show composition and growth regions.

either end. In the center there is a sort of race between cells laying down bone and cells chomping it up Pac man style; this activity leaves spongy central regions. It lightens the bone and creates the region called bone marrow, where blood cells are formed.

The same sort of chase is occurring in separate regions on each end. The area between the "growing ends" and the "growing center" is called the epiphyseal plate or growth plate.

This is the region in kids' bones of very active growth, or laying down of new bone. The gap narrows as they get older until it's just a line when they are done growing. When this occurs, we say that the "growth plate has fused," which can be confirmed by X-ray. The precise timing is different in each kid, but it follows a predictable order once puberty begins. On average, the beginning of growth plate fusion occurs in girls from ages 12–14 and in boys from 14–16, although they may continue to grow in height into their twenties.

Because of the soft nature of the new bone, growth plates are quite susceptible to injury. Damage or displacement in the growth plate region can be particularly dangerous for a young person. Athletes with injured growth plates either left untreated or poorly treated risk permanent impairment. The wise coach treats even the risk of any such injury with this firmly in mind.

Skeletal growth and change is quite dynamic, especially during certain periods known as growth spurts. Active growth requires plentiful building materials, so a healthy diet with sufficient protein, vitamins and minerals is essential. Keep in mind that, while healthy bodies build strong bones, undernourished bodies run the risk of having weaker, more brittle bones. Even kids who eat plenty of calories may be undernourished if their foods are not nutrient-dense. It's where "you are what you eat" rings very true. Weight-bearing exercise that stimulates bone formation in all the right places calls on this nourishment to build healthy athletes.

Joints

Without joints we couldn't move. Movement happens when a muscle that spans a joint contracts with enough force to pull one bone toward another. The range of motion allowed at a joint is a function of the shape of the two bones that come together. Joints come in different varieties and may be grouped into the kinds of motion they allow. Two main categories of interest for soccer athletes are:

- Hinge joints that allow bending like the hinge of a door; movement at these joints is called flexion or extension; elbows, knees and ankles are modified hinges
- Ball and socket joints in which the rounded head of one bone fits into the rounded depression in the other bone, allowing a much broader range of motion; to flexion and extension they add abduction, adduction, rotation and circumduction; examples are shoulders and hips

We need our joints to be both flexible and stable—flexible enough to allow for smooth movement through a full range of motion, but stable enough to track properly and remain firm against the strong pull of surrounding muscles or the push of external forces. Some joints, like elbows and hips, are structurally stable because of the good "fit" between the bones and taut ligaments holding them in place. In a healthy body these are rarely injured, except in the case of trauma.

However, some joints, like knees, cause trouble where the "fit" of the bones is not very secure. One bone seems just to balance on the other.

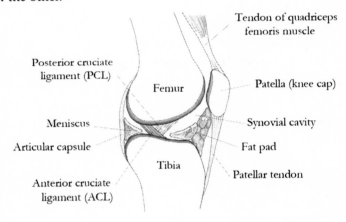

Figure 2. Section through the knee joint. A complex hinge formed by the femur and tibia, traversed by the patella and supported and protected by ligaments, cartilage and joint capsule.

The design seems poorly suited for walking upright, let alone running. A special cushioning disc called a meniscus that rests atop the tibia helps to increase the surface area in contact and deepen the articulation to improve the "fit." Also, crisscrossing ligaments inside the joint capsule and strap-like ligaments to the sides assist in holding the bones in place. Still, structural stability is low, and sports that demand dynamic movement at the knee challenge its integrity. Balanced strength of the surrounding muscles and the tendons as they cross the joint is essential to support and stabilize it and allow for safe movement.

Young children usually have full range of motion at all their joints and don't require extra flexibility training, although teaching them the stretches early, when they are easy to do, introduces the tools to address the tightness that may come later. (Caution: children with range of motion well beyond normal may require extra strengthening to protect those joints.) When kids begin their growth spurts, their bones grow in length more quickly than the muscles can stretch to keep up across the joints. Kids have newly longer limbs and much tighter muscles, even at rest. Motion may be awkward and poorly coordinated. A friend called this her daughter's "giraffe stage"; that describes it well. Insist on a regular stretching routine with these athletes to develop their flexibility. (See chapter 5 for details.)

If you work with both boys and girls, you may notice differences in flexibility between the two groups. Hormone differences contribute to the apparent gender disparities in flexibility and strength in post-pubertal youth players. Females tend to be slightly more flexible; males tend to have greater muscle mass. So the challenges of "joint health" in the sexes are slightly different. Fortunately, our joints respond to both strength and flexibility training, which are not mutually exclusive. One look at Olympic gymnasts of either gender will prove that joints can be both strong and flexible if trained to be that way.

Connective Tissue

We keep those bones in line at the joints with fibrous connective tissue as follows:

- Cartilage: lining the outer surfaces at the ends of the long bones at the joints to prevent friction during movement (the meniscus, mentioned above, is composed of a specialized type of cartilage)
- Ligaments: connecting bone to bone, sometimes within a joint capsule (the anterior cruciate ligament, or ACL, is an example) but often in fibrous cords traversing joints on all sides
- Tendons: attaching muscle to bone, extending from the fibrous covering of the muscle and transmitting the active force to move the bone

If you have been around sports for long, you are familiar with cartilage, ligaments and tendons, probably mentioned in the same breath with injury. They are in the "line of fire," at work and under stress whenever the body is moving. Connective tissue serves its purpose well. It is highly mobile and flexible because it's very fibrous, but it's not as strong as bone (so it tears) and it has little to no blood supply (so it repairs itself poorly if at all). While broken bones do recover from breaks because they have good blood circulation, cartilage and ligaments generally don't. Thus, significant injuries to these require surgical repair.

Like bone, connective tissue is active, dynamic tissue, but it doesn't have the complex nutrient supply system that bone has. Instead, it generally relies on nutrients to diffuse in from the surrounding fluids. Joint movement squeezes and releases these tissues, like a sponge, moving fluid and nourishment in and out, thus lubricating the internal workings like oil for the engine. This is the primary reason why it is essential to isolate joint movements in your warm-up and insist on movement through the whole range of motion. Warmed synovial fluid seeps into all the joint spaces, facilitating smooth and supple movement. Cold joints are stiff and tentative; thus, failure to warm up increases the chance of a pulled muscle. It is also why recovering range of motion (ROM) in a previously injured joint is the first step toward return to health and return to play.

Muscles

Muscles are our engine; they allow us to move. Skeletal muscles work together to activate voluntary movement of body parts at our various joints. Skeletal muscles have a magical design and complex organization so precise that through regular exacting practice, they can be trained to execute the most detailed maneuvers or the largest, most spectacular feats.

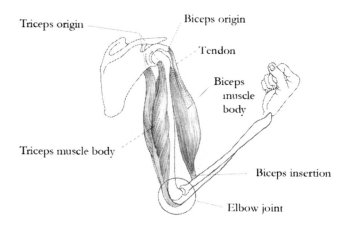

Figure 3. The elbow joint. Contraction of the biceps muscle flexes the elbow. Contraction of the triceps muscle extends the elbow.

Don't know muscle design? You know more than you think. Unless you're a vegetarian, you've probably been asked, "dark meat or white?" That's a choice between types of skeletal muscle fiber types. Tear off the skin of a drumstick and you can see the fantastic design of the typical skeletal muscle—elongated, elastic structures attached by tendons to bones. Skeletal muscles generally have two sites of attachment, one more proximal (closer to the body center), called the origin, and the other more distal (further from the body), called the insertion.

In a typical contraction, the origin remains fixed and the insertion moves toward it along the line of muscle pull. The joint between them provides the axis around which movement occurs.

Muscle tissue is specialized to respond to nervous stimulation by contracting. The electrical signal sent via nerve is transmitted to individual muscle fibers which make up the muscle. This initiates an amazing sequence of events. Tiny fibrils, using energy inside the cells, slide past one another and pull the ends of the muscle toward its center. The proportion of muscle fibers activated in a given contraction depends on the "instructions" received from the brain, the commander of the nervous system. This allows for a gradual, orderly and appropriate response depending on the task. Lots of fibers for the free kick from midfield. Fewer fibers for the delicate flick. Each, according to plan.

In large body movements, muscles act in muscle groups rather than individually. These teams of muscles have assigned responsibilities, grouped according to their contributions to a particular motion:

- Prime mover: the muscle supplying the greatest force in the movement
- Agonists and/or synergists: muscles working with the prime mover to contribute additional force
- Antagonists: muscles whose contraction opposes the agonists; they must be relaxed to allow the designated motion to proceed at full force, but their gradual activation is what slows the agonist motion already in progress
- Stabilizers: muscles providing support by contracting to prevent unwanted movement or to hold the non-moving parts in place

Obviously, a simple motion at a joint is not really so simple, especially weight-bearing motion, which requires the contribution of postural muscles and stabilizers throughout. Add to this the timing in a movement pattern and the gradation of force required, and you have quite a complex series of signals and responses. Stage fright is a familiar phenomenon of this system gone wrong, where the body's response to fear or indecision confuses this array of signals, and a co-contraction of opposing muscles actually makes movement impossible. This adrenaline overload may also contribute to the delay in pulling the trigger in a tense moment on the field.

Contractions that shorten muscle fibers and result in motion are called isotonic contractions. Not all muscle contractions cause muscle shortening. A muscle may generate contractile force but actually be lengthened by the pull of an opposing muscle or in opposition to gravity. Contraction of this type is called eccentric (lengthening) contraction. This is especially important to control the rate of activated movements and contain the range of motion. For instance, the lengthening of the hamstring muscle slows the forceful extension of the knee in the kicking motion, preventing hyperextension injury. The thigh muscles contract eccentrically to control the body as it lowers in a squat or to prepare for a jump. Performed slowly, this lengthening stores energy for release in the resulting spring upward.

Finally, isometric (non-shortening or same length) contractions generate force insufficient to overcome resistance, so no movement occurs. Muscles contracting to stabilize a body part are one example. Postural muscles are constantly contracting to hold us upright, even without our conscious instructions. In fact, all healthy muscle has a relay of stimulating signal traveling to it that results in what we know as "muscle tone." Regular exercise increases this resting stimulation, making fit people not only look healthier but also more ready to call muscles into action. Warm-up also activates this neuromuscular connection, readying the body for activity.

Now you realize that the notion that only one muscle is responsible for each movement is far from the truth. A group of muscles prepares the joint, while a sequence of muscles acts to accomplish a desired motion at a designated pace with a prescribed amount of control. The athletic movements on the field are more complex yet. They involve continuous give and take among muscles, joints and various body sensors (discussed below) to coordinate changes in position as the game, the surface and the opponent demand. Even the "simple" striking motion of a penalty kick requires an elaborate sequence of muscle activation at hip, knee, ankle and foot, continuously changing throughout preparation, strike and follow through.

Of course, all this movement would be ineffective without a stabilized core against which to pull. This is often overlooked but can be demonstrated with a simple example. Picture a kid getting ready to jump from the dock into the lake. Now, think about what would happen if the dock were unsecured. The dock would slip backward as the kid attempted to propel himself forward. He would not go very far from the dock, and hopefully there would be no injuries. For an effective jump, the dock has to be stabilized. For effective limb movement, the torso has to be stabilized. Stabilizing muscles in the abdomen, chest, back and shoulders secure the dock, so to speak.

Indeed, any time we intend to move, we must first subconsciously activate stabilizing muscles to fix the non-moving parts against which the moving parts pull. They need to be fully prepared to resist the strong pull of the prime mover muscle(s). When they are not, movement is weakened, off-balance, ineffective or disabled. This is why strengthening of the "core" muscles of the body is so important. These are the muscles of the torso against which all limb muscles pull to accomplish movement.

Muscle Energetics

Muscles require energy to do the work they do. Understanding a bit about energy demands, energy sources and the capacity of the various supply systems will help you design your most effective soccer workouts.

At the cellular level, the muscles derive energy from a molecule called adenosine triphosphate, or ATP. Thousands of ATPs split every second in working muscle. Because of this huge demand, resting muscles have only about two seconds worth of ATP on hand to use for immediate work. Conveniently, another system, using creatine phosphate, can be activated to provide some additional quick ATP, but only enough for another 15 seconds or so. Not much when you have a 90-minute game to play, right?

So the soccer player generally makes use of two additional larger capacity energy systems to supply working muscles during play.

- Anaerobic glycolysis: quick energy is produced from the breakdown of glycogen stored in the muscle. The process is anaerobic because it doesn't rely on a ready supply of oxygen, but it "costs" the muscle cell an accumulation of lactic acid that builds up in the blood stream, causing fatigue. This pathway supplies energy for about 120 additional seconds of peak exertion.
- Aerobic respiration: provides enough energy to sustain effort for extended time at submaximal exertion levels, but only if there is sufficient oxygen delivery to the working muscles. The steps in this pathway take some time to get into gear, but once they do, the aerobic system is an efficient and reliable source of energy.

Because soccer requires both submaximal energy expenditure (jogging, tracking, marking, etc.) and bouts of near peak usage (attacking, sprinting, countering), players need to call on both anaerobic and aerobic energy systems. Submaximal efforts can be sustained over a long period of time, at least until the body's stores of glycogen are used up. In a well-prepared athlete, this may be two hours or more. Few experience the total depletion thought to cause the "hitting the wall" phenomenon that disables marathon runners after several hours of running. It shouldn't be a limiting factor for a well-fed soccer player, though it may be a consideration on tournament weekends where multiple game efforts may have a cumulative depleting effect.

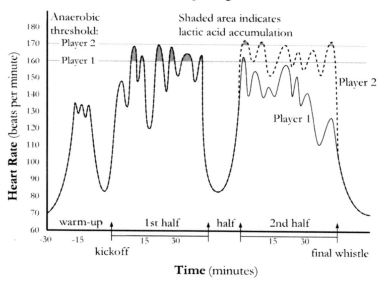

Figure 4. Anaerobic threshold shift as player becomes more fit. If Players 1 and 2 have similar exertion in the first half, Player 1 (anaerobic threshold at 160 bpm) has 6 efforts that accumulate lactic acid, whereas Player 2 (anaerobic threshold at 170 bpm) has no such efforts. In the second half, Player 1 shows fatigued play, whereas Player 2 continues to perform at a high level.

On the other hand, anaerobic processes are fatiguing. They lead to metabolite buildup and put the body into what is known as "oxygen debt." They produce quick energy inefficiently, and in order to recover, the body responds with increased breathing to take in more oxygen to replace what was spent. When a soccer player is bent over catching his breath, he is not playing his best soccer.

The key, then, is to train the aerobic system to provide energy for the entire game and to train the anaerobic system for the bouts of peak demand that occur during the game. An athlete who can stay in his aerobic zone for all but the most strenuous efforts will experience less fatigue and require less recovery. Conditioning key: doing a quantity of training at or near anaerobic threshold (the workload at which the energy supply shifts from aerobic to anaerobic sources) raises an athlete's anaerobic threshold. That means he will stay in the aerobic zone longer and delay fatigue, allowing him to play stronger for longer—a winning combination.

The Neuromuscular Connection

Voluntary movement and its coordination do not happen by accident. Your nervous system is in charge. It plans action, signals the message, receives positional information and recalibrates at lightning speed. Bundles of nerve fibers extend from your brain to all parts of your body. Those that innervate muscles are called motor neurons. Electrical signals travel both to and from the muscles. Those headed "to" the muscle tell it what to do, how fast, in what order, with what sequence and when to stop. Those coming "from" the muscle bring sensory information telling the brain what the muscle is doing. Sensory information also comes from the joints and tendons with "positional" information. Try this: with your arm behind your back, bend your elbow at 90 degrees and use a mirror to see how close you got to a right angle. How do you know how to do this? You can "feel" it. That's proprioception, the body's movement sensation. Athletes count on this.

Of course, when you are new to an activity, it is hard. You need to look at what you are doing, adding visual feedback to the information provided by the joints and muscles. But each time you do it, you are teaching your body what it feels like to move in a particular way. This is why it's essential to practice proper form and technique from the start. As they say, practice doesn't make perfect; only perfect practice makes perfect.

Practice reinforces the neuromuscular pathways, the signaling and sensory pathways for movement from the brain to the muscles and back. This is what is known as muscle memory. Getting lots of ball touches and repeating a skill many times adds to this memory. We can see this "memorizing" process take place in our junior soccer players as they begin to get their first touches on the ball. Where are their eyes? Glued to the ball. When they start to "feel" the ball, they gain confidence to direct their eyes elsewhere.

In very advanced players the brain-to-muscle connection may appear nearly automatic. We see this in many skilled sports when an athlete is "in the zone," or "playing out of his head." His action-response happens more fluidly or more quickly or more accurately than could possibly happen via the typical nerve-to-muscle activation pathways we've described. Sport scientists suspect that these neuromuscular patterns have been "chunked" or saved in the motor-memory file as patterned responses, then called upon as a unit rather than as individual signals, with little to no central activation. It's almost instinctual.

Much of what your body does is programmed in, happening automatically without your thinking about it. Your heart beats. You breathe, digest, process food and waste, etc. All of this is regulated below the level of the "conscious" mind by brain centers dedicated to these tasks. While most skeletal muscle movement is voluntary (your brain tells your body to move), there are involuntary movements called reflexes that happen without conscious thought. They are "pre-programmed" connections between a nerve and a muscle, usually for the protection of the body. Common examples are pulling your finger back from a hot stove or throwing your hand up to shield your face from an incoming ball. Unfortunately, sometimes even reflexive movement cannot happen quickly enough.

One reflex coaches should be aware of is the stretch reflex. Designed to protect the muscle from a sudden dangerous overstretch, a quickly stretched muscle automatically initiates its own strong reflexive contraction. A slow, sustained stretch does not activate this reflex. This is why ballistic (bouncing) stretches are ineffective in developing flexibility. Sport scientists recommend that a stretch be performed slowly and sustained for at least 20–30 seconds to be effective. This practice prevents activation of the stretch reflex and allows the muscle to lengthen. (See chapter 5 for more on proper stretching.)

The Heart of the Matter

None of the body's systems can function without the constant delivery of oxygen and nutrients to working tissues and the removal of waste products from them. This is accomplished by the circulatory system, which is powered by the heart. Blood-borne nutrients and oxygen are delivered via a complex array of arteries to capillaries in the tissues. There, they are exchanged for carbon dioxide and metabolic waste products that are whisked away to the junk-processing depots of the body.

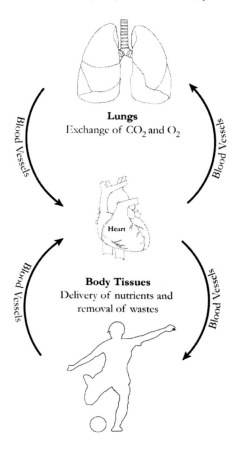

Lungs
Exchange of CO_2 and O_2

Blood Vessels

Blood Vessels

Heart

Blood Vessels

Body Tissues
Delivery of nutrients and removal of wastes

Blood Vessels

Figure 5. The circulatory system

Cardiovascular (heart and blood vessel) training is typically referred to by coaches and trainers as "fitness training" or conditioning. It enhances sport performance by virtue of changes to the heart muscle itself, the volume and capacity of the blood circulation and efficiency of exchange of nutrients and metabolites in the working tissues. Added together, cardio training can help athletes make substantial strides in increased endurance.

In brief, the well-trained athlete has these cardiovascular advantages:

- The heart muscle is a more efficient pump, circulating more blood per beat at a lower energy cost.
- More circulating hemoglobin increases the capacity to carry oxygen to working muscle tissue and remove carbon dioxide from it; additional hemoglobin also enhances oxygen exchange from the lungs.
- Increased gradients across the tissues for extraction of oxygen delivered and removal of carbon dioxide excreted mean that muscles can work at a higher intensity without the buildup of fatiguing metabolites. This delays the shift to the inefficient "high gear."
- Greater muscle tone in the extremities increases venous return to the heart, decreasing the energy cost of circulation and enhancing the volume the heart pumps.
- Trained muscles operate economically, efficient in recruiting the right proportion and type of muscle fibers, conserving energy and reducing wasted energy expenditure.

In addition, we know regular training causes adaptations in skeletal muscle on the cellular level, which enhances performance. The engine starts to purr. Coordination and balance improve as the athlete adopts familiar movement patterns and streamlines movements; this makes him more fuel-efficient and his movement smoother.

Once you've tuned the engine, lubricated the gears and perfected the timing, be sure you tell them not to rev the engine. Adrenaline overdrive is a big energy waster. Once they fasten adrenaline overdrive firmly in the passenger seat, they're ready for the green light. But it's a long way to the finish line. The rest of this book will show you how to help them get there, and maybe even take checkered flag.

3

Fitness Prescription
for Sports:
Meeting the Demands

We know what we want to train, and we have the background to train it, but how will we make the time? You're a coach with a team, or you're a parent with an athlete, and there is a game to play, but you're maxed out already on available time for fitness training. Fortunately, the game helps us out here in several ways. Because it is a demanding game, your hard-working players will be training for fitness while they're working on soccer, even though it's not everything they need or quite that simple. And while the game does not provide all the fitness they require, it does identify the fitness improvements our players need. You can see their lagging fitness from the sidelines.

- They get shoved off the ball—they need core strength and balance.
- They lose the footrace to the ball—they need sprint speed and quickness.
- Their feet are leaden in the second half—they need endurance conditioning.
- They try the shot with their weaker foot and it dribbles to the keeper—they need targeted strength and coordination in the performance of the skill.

The game itself saves us time by handing us opportunities to identify our players' weaknesses, but just playing the game is not enough to strengthen them progressively. This chapter gives you tools to create the training needed. We'll walk through the principles of training fitness for soccer and other sports with similar physical demands (basketball, lacrosse, field hockey, volleyball) and identify how these principles can be applied to progress your players from where they are to where they are willing to go. That's what coaching is all about. A coach is meant to carry people to their destination. When we can be this vehicle for young athletes, we are giving them a great gift and introducing them to a lifelong practice.

A heads up before we begin:

- Athletes must be physiologically and psychologically ready for the training to benefit from it. Readiness comes with maturation. Match your training to the brains and bodies you have.

- Athletes are individuals. Their responses to training will vary. Expect and allow for this.
- Adaptation to training takes time. Designing a program with gradual progression is essential. Regular variation in the challenges presented keeps things fresh.

Ground rules: Overload According to FITS

Physical training requires application of the overload principle (not to be confused with "overtraining," which we will discuss more later). That is, the body's systems need to do more than they're used to or be "overloaded" in order to get stronger. Overload doesn't mean just doing the same thing over and over again and expecting new results. (See Webster's definition of insanity.) The overload principle requires that we subject bodies to change in quantity, quality or type of training to expect improvement. The principle of overload applies to all sorts of training. As a healthy body responds to the increased demand, it adapts and readies to accommodate future demands.

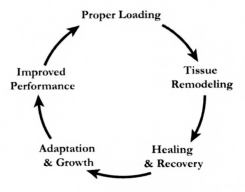

Figure 6. Cycle of training adaptation

Progressive overload training stimulates all of the systems the body calls on during physical performance: muscles, nerves, heart, lungs. This demand results in immediate increases in output coupled with long-term changes that occur at a cellular level. The key is providing gradual but challenging demands.

Of course, this varies from system to system and athlete to athlete, and can be tough for the coach attempting to challenge all players despite individual variation in abilities and preparation. One good way to approach this is to apply step-wise goals based on the percentage of improvement from an individual baseline performance (e.g., a goal of 10% improvement in juggles is 10 more for a player who can already do 100, but only 1 more for a player who can do 10). This works equally well for clocked time in a 40m sprint or a 2K run. Each player's target time is relative to last season or to their personal best time.

The rate of improvement in fitness has been shown to be related to three factors and a principle. The factors are *Frequency*, *Intensity*, and *Time* (duration); related to these is *Specificity*. We'll use the acronym FITS to remember them.

- Frequency is how often you perform a specified kind of training: daily, 3X/week, weekly, monthly, etc. Proper frequency depends on the body's ability to recover from a bout of training because adaptation must occur before the system can be safely challenged again without risking injury, exhaustion and burnout.

- Intensity is the load or demand of the physical training. A body experiences greater overload with high intensity training but cannot sustain that performance level for very long. Lower intensity training is less taxing and can be sustained longer. Balancing intensity with proper recovery is essential. The muscles adapt differently to differing intensities, so training design should imitate sport demands.

- **T**ime is the duration of training, specifically how long a body system is challenged; hours/day, days/week, etc. Too many minutes of high intensity training and competitive play is a recipe for overtraining and injury. Pay close attention to the ratio of training/play minutes and time to recover. Good training is designed to prepare the body for competition. Competition will subject young bodies and minds to high intensity stressors for the duration.

- **S**pecificity is simple. You improve only what you train: the energy system, the muscles, the joints, the bones. Choose what you desire to train and design your fitness with that in mind. Aerobic conditioning does not add much strength to muscles. Shooting with the right foot does little for the left-footed shot. Intense training of one system or one muscle group selectively exhausts the body, so be smart about varying your training.

Progression (make haste slowly)

For the body to achieve healthy adaptation and growth, training must follow a prescribed pattern of gradual progression using the FITS elements. Demanding too much too quickly from a body breaks it down. Without adequate time for recovery, adaptation and growth cannot occur. Ignoring recovery is likely to result in injury, so patience in training is essential. The only way to sustain and build on gains is to follow the pattern: challenge/recover/ challenge+. The recovery period doesn't need to be complete rest, but it must offer sufficient recovery to the system that is rebuilding.

For coaches who meet their teams daily, soccer cross-training is essential. By this I mean intentionally planning to rest on day 2 what you trained hard on day 1. For example, if you worked on short sprints and plyometrics for anaerobic conditioning on Monday, schedule gentle jogging and technical play on Tuesday. Important caution: identify the players who play for more than one team in the same season. For the health of these players, make every effort to connect with the other coach to communicate about their practice plans and competition schedules so the physical demands made on the player are manageable.

For coaches of younger players or recreational players, the frequency of training sessions may be predetermined by the coordinators who make field assignments. You may meet 2–3 times per week and have a game on the weekends. This schedule offers rest days that your players need. Keep in mind, though, that multi-game and tournament weekends are demanding. It should be obvious that it is unwise to subject players to a physically demanding practice the day before a game, though tuning up and technical play with the team can be good.

The day after, let 'em rest. Unfortunately, I have heard of too many coaches who, discontent with players' performance on the weekend, "punish" their players with fitness on Monday. There is NO PLACE in youth sports for punishment fitness. We want kids to enjoy their sports experience and learn to use their bodies well, not abuse them. Punishment conditioning is abuse; it's about the coach's anger, and it must be stopped. Any instances of this should be reported to the organizing bodies, league administrators or officials who can take appropriate action.

How do I progress my players safely and effectively? For soccer, which requires varied bouts of intense effort interspersed with active recovery (walking, jogging), interval training can mirror the demands of play and is a great way to enhance fitness. As mentioned in chapter 2, the advantage goes to players who can perform at a higher level for longer. This requires training at or near their anaerobic (or lactate) threshold with the intention of pushing this threshold higher. Because high intensity effort is fatiguing, recovery is necessary. It should be active to assist in removing lactic acid from working muscle tissue.

Interval training is prescribed by the time and distance of the work interval, the length of the rest period between bouts and the total number of repetitions performed—e.g., running 4 x 120 yards (the length of a full-size field) in 20 seconds and jogging back in 45 seconds with a 15 second rest gives 1 minute recovery between reps. The percent effort and the primary energy system trained for intervals of different lengths are described in the chart below. The time expectations will depend on your athletes and their abilities. Time can be modified as they improve in fitness, but here are some interval recommendations:

Interval Training Prescription					
Interval	System Trained	Reps	Duration	Work/Rest Ratio	% Effort
Long	Anaerobic threshold	4-6	2-5 min	1:1[†]	70-80
Medium	Glycogen pathway	8-12	60-90 s	1:2	80-90
Short	High energy	15-20	30-60 s	1:3[‡]	95
Sprint	Speed	25+	10-30 s	1:3	100
[†] 1:1 means rest duration = work duration					
[‡] 1:3 means rest duration = 3x work duration					

As you can see, these are high intensity demands. Your athletes will be breathing heavily after each effort. Recovery should be sufficient before the next rep. Sport scientists teach athletes to pace themselves by monitoring their recovery heart rates and taking extra recovery time if their heart rate has not recovered to an established level. This may or may not be workable with your players, but a good gauge is this: if they are chatting with their neighbors, they have too much recovery. Still, performing tough intervals is more fun when you do it in a group or as part of a game or competition, complete with reinforcing feedback. Distraction is bliss. But don't mess with their heads and add "one more" to punish after requiring 100% effort on the last interval. Who are you punishing most? The one who actually just gave you 100%, the one you want to reward.

Caution: be careful about running intervals based not on the clock but on the number of players in line (i.e., "You go when you're the next player in line."). This inadvertently burdens the kids in the "short" line or all the kids on a day when you have players absent but keep the same number of lines. It makes medium rest intervals into short ones, and kids can't get enough recovery. When you are unsure, always err on the side of more rest. Keep it fun and the kids will enjoy it more. Keep it varied as well. Remember, effort doesn't have to be just running. High intensity activities like hopping, bounding, skipping, crab crawling, etc., can break things up. (See chapter 4 for ways to add fun to your fitness.) They're fun and they use different muscle groups, which gives you some cross training in your intervals. Now that's good planning and smart coaching.

How do I know when to push and when to pull back? Some of this, honestly, is trial and error. You know your team and your players. Be wary of using either the fittest player or the least fit to set intensity and rest intervals. Your objective is to provide a challenge to all of your players, but the bigger the range, the harder this is. Your goal is to help your athletes learn to feel the level they are working at and to motivate them to push themselves. Some will. Some won't. The ones who will do it get better faster. That is their reward. The others will still benefit but won't progress as quickly. It is actually the ones in the middle, the "swing players," where you can have the most influence. They may have never challenged themselves and aren't aware of what they can do. If you are encouraging, they will give "tough" a try, and their stronger bodies will be both their reward and their increased motivation for next time. If you're really lucky, the weaker players will be watching and find motivation in these as well.

Overtraining and moderation. Occasionally we are blessed with a player who comes as a complete motivation package. There is no stopping them. You gotta love this—until they get hurt. This highly motivated athlete comes in at least two forms: (1) gives her all physically and (2) gives her all emotionally. The first can be a train wreck on the field. Her fearlessness can result in great play, especially because other players may step back in self-preservation or respect, but it can also result in undisciplined play, which is unsafe for her, her teammates and her opponents. Your responsibility as coach is to rein in this player and expect smart, disciplined play while encouraging enthusiasm and effort.

The player who gives herself emotionally may be your "go-to" player for pressure situations. She may be a team leader or captain. She always leaves it all on the field. You don't ever have to motivate her to work harder. She will raise the motivation level of the team. The coaching challenge with her is to moderate the negative emotions, such as anger, disappointment or fear of failure. We know that sometimes effort and energy are not enough to win the day; this player needs help seeing that no matter the outcome, her effort today was essential to the team. The coaching challenge is to celebrate the emotional leadership on winning days while moderating the emotional damage on losing days, so that what seems like failure today serves as motivation, not fear, for next time.

For the majority of players, fitness training intensity can be monitored in one of three ways:

- The "talk test" (mentioned above), easy conversation that means they are working at below target training level
- Perceived exertion, self-measured and monitored by them at your instruction to "do this one at __% effort" (see chart above). Keep in mind that a less fit kid may be last to finish but still be working at a high % perceived exertion.
- Recovery heart rate. This is the most physiological but requires players to stop and count their pulse during training. It can be measured at the wrist or carotid artery. Count this for 10 seconds and multiply by 6, or count for 15 seconds and multiply by 4 to get beats/minute. Exercise heart rates will vary. (See Appendix A to learn how to calculate the target heart rate.)

Overtraining is an important concern for young athletes today; avoid it. While you want training to be effective, pushing too hard runs the risk of injury, and for nonprofessional and youth athletes this is a risk not worth taking. When a kid loses interest, doesn't want to go to practice, is fatigued, isn't eating or is angry or depressed, he may be burned out. Check for overtraining. (See Appendix B for a more complete list of signs of burnout and ways to prevent it.)

You can be in the prevention business by planning your training sessions with rest and recovery in mind. In addition, help your players become aware of their own daily stress levels. The gold standard for measuring the stress on the body is the resting heart rate, taken daily, before getting out of bed in the morning. I instruct players to keep paper and pen by their bed and count and record their 60-second heart rate. An excuse to lie there for another minute! Making a note if it shows spikes or a pattern trending upward is an excellent way for any individual to become aware that his or her body is under stress. This is not just limited to physical stress; tests and late night studying, boyfriend and girlfriend drama, poor eating, dehydration, family tenseness and illness are other ways the body can be stressed. The body responds the same way to any stressor—by going on full alert. Heart rate and respirations will be elevated even "at rest." This means that players arrive at practice already well on their way to their training heart rate. Getting to know your players off the field as well as on is the best way to help them with life's stresses. When you recognize the signs of stress, don't have them push it. The fact that they're out there with the team may be the best thing for their day. Leave improvements in fitness for another day.

A special case: Returning to play/coming back from injury and the deconditioning effect. More and more, we are seeing kids getting hurt on the field of play. Why this is happening is the subject of much debate in the sports medicine realm. As a coach, though, you must deal effectively with two decision challenges: (1) same game return to play and (2) post-injury de-training and return to play progression.

- Same game: If you are fortunate enough to have a health professional (athletic trainer, physician) available to do the assessment on the field, great, though most coaches as first responders have to make this call themselves on a regular basis. If there is any question of an injury to the head, take the kid out. Insist that they have their injury assessed as soon as possible. Do not let them return to play until they are cleared by a medical professional. If their injury seems minor, talk to the player and have them move around. If they can execute the skills required for play at the pace demanded, smoothly and with no interruption, I let them return to play if they wish. If movement is hindered or hitched in any way, I take them out until they can move smoothly: next half, next game, or after they have been evaluated and cleared to play.
- Post-injury: When a player has been out of practice and play for a length of time but has been cleared to play, the situation for the coach is different. Be aware that de-training will have occurred in this athlete. Fitness and strength decline somewhat in the time off from play, and significantly if the athlete has been on crutches or

otherwise immobilized. He will need some time to return to previous physical form for fitness, skill, coordination and balance. Observe his progress in all these areas. If he has worked with a physical therapist and/or a physical trainer, that person can provide extremely valuable recommendations for return and progression.

Caution: Especially at higher performance levels, players returning after significant injury will likely suffer injury to their confidence as well as their fitness. They may not realize this until they jump back in. They need to be reintroduced to contact play slowly, to regain confidence that they can perform without getting injured. One good way to do this is to have them wear a "no pressure" pinny. Get them used to moving without contact; then allow them to request to take off the pinny when they feel they are ready to return to full contact play.

Is fitness fun or is it work? When a coach announces "we're gonna do fitness today," I have observed teams respond with groans and grimaces. These players have been introduced to fitness by a coach who sees fitness as a chore—necessary work, but absolute drudgery. He sets aside particular practice days for "work" and no "play." Who wants to do that? It should come as no surprise to this coach when his players turn up missing on "fitness day." Too much homework, chores, any excuse will do. If coaches want players to embrace the fitness component of their preparation for the game, they need to blend it with the game. Make it play. Make it fun.

But wait. At the beginning of this chapter we said that the game doesn't provide all the fitness players need. Yes, we can't count on it to do fitness for us. Instead, the smart coach uses the game to identify the technical, tactical and fitness objectives for his players. Rather than separating these (and who has time to do all three separately?), create ways to work the components of fitness into regular practice activities: warm-up, skills, drills, scrimmages and cool-down. Remember that fitness done as a team, in competition against ourselves or our teammates, for reward, even if it's only the favorite color pinny, by invitation and with expectation, creates kids who may choose fitness for the rest of their lives. Don't you want that for your kids?

Don't fall for the fitness fallacies. Here are a few popular fitness fallacies and misconceptions we need to dispel before we go further. On the true/false test, *mark all of these false.*

1. *No pain, no gain.* (**false**) While training can be difficult and sometimes uncomfortable, it shouldn't hurt. Pain is not a natural consequence of exercise or training; it is a signal from the body that should not be ignored. While high intensity training may result in sore muscles and fatigue, if the athletes are in pain, the training is probably excessive. Never require a young athlete in pain to continue. You would never knowingly do this, right? But don't even imply it. Especially for boys, don't belittle a player who may be in pain by calling him weak or wimpy, and monitor this ribbing among players on the team. Especially for girls, don't celebrate the player who finished the game on a sprained ankle. Girls will get the idea that this is what you're looking for and fail to

report a minor injury before it gets full blown. Don't play through pain, ever.

2. *Muscle turns to fat or vice versa.* (**false**) Nope, and I hope you're laughing with me. One tissue type is not converted to another. Each is a unique tissue type with unique characteristics: muscle has long, thin fibers that are excitable and can convert energy to movement; fat has large globular cells designed to store adipose tissue. Exercise can increase the size of muscle fibers (hypertrophy) and inactivity can reduce them (atrophy). Excess calorie consumption grows fat cells. A negative energy balance (burning more calories than you take in) can deplete their stores, though it does not reduce their number. Often people who are very active consume many calories in support of their activity; when they stop exercising, if they don't reduce calorie consumption accordingly, they will fill those fat cells up. Doubly insulting as they watch their muscles shrink and their muscle tone fade.

3. *Spot reducing for weight loss.* (**false**) Especially if you coach girls, some if not most of them will be looking to reduce some part of their body they deem over-large. This is a tough conversation, particularly for a male coach, because eating behavior is an emotionally charged topic. Disordered eating is prevalent, particularly among high-achieving athletic women. (See chapter 6 for healthy nutrition practices.) The truth for weight loss is this: last place on, first place off, and vice versa. That means that people tend to store extra fat in a predictable and ordered way. Even very thin individuals will have stingy spots

that hang on to fat stores. The healthy way to approach weight issues with athletes is to keep the conversation geared toward performance and health. Bodies that are fed in a healthy and responsible way perform better on the field. Let that be their motivation to take care of their nutrition. If an athlete has a significant weight issue, he or she should be referred to a sports nutritionist.

4. *I'm running out of wind, so give me oxygen!* **(false)** This is a fallacy reinforced by professional football players on the sidelines on TV. Even at very high exertion rates our blood oxygen levels change very little because the blood has a large carrying capacity for oxygen. There is plenty of oxygen in "regular" air to supply all the athlete needs. Breathing pure oxygen does not provide any physical advantage. Breathing through that mask may give a psychological boost, but so can a good pep talk. Train regularly so your athletes are aware of what that lactate threshold feels like, and they'll know how to gauge their effort.

See Appendices:

A. Target Heart Rate: How to calculate and use to gauge training intensity

B. Overtraining: Signs, Symptoms and Prevention

4

Fitting Fitness into the Practice Plan

oaches have limited time to meet with their teams, and much of that time must be dedicated to skills training and team play. Few coaches have discretionary time to include fitness, so they add it at the expense of technical work. With planning and creativity, fitness training can be applied during regular soccer sessions. This helps kids see both the game and the fitness as part of the game, instead of play first, then workout. In this chapter we'll use the framework of a typical practice plan and outline how best to blend the fitness they need into sport-specific drills, skills and games.

So, fitting in fitness without taking any additional time sounds attractive, but you're skeptical. Don't be. You do it all the time, only you call it multitasking. Think about it as intentionally multitasking. I sometimes call it the "Life Cereal" approach to youth sports because you're getting them to do something that's good for them in a way that "tastes good." But don't tell them, or they might not eat it. This will be our secret. But it's way more than trickery, isn't it? This subterfuge serves a positive purpose.

As a coach you are operating amidst collision forces. On a regular day at practice this is your to-do list:

- Develop player skills
- Increase physical fitness
- Unite the team while teaching good sportsmanship
- Grow competitiveness
- Field a team with the ability to win
- And, oh yeah, have fun.

That's a pretty tall order. But as coach that's what you've signed on for. At least, that's what the parents will tell you at the beginning of the season. When we formed our travel team, my team parents filled out a survey about their interest in the team. This was the essay question: "What would you and your family like for your child to get out of the travel soccer experience?" The bulleted list above was repeated on nearly every sheet.

But how do you do all this when you've got them only a few hours per week? When they're younger, players and their parents look to you to make most of this happen. You can achieve it—even the fun part—if you have a practice plan and are willing to be flexible with it. When they're older, you still need the practice plan, but flexibility means a willingness to hand them some of the responsibility for their own achievement or lack of it. This give-and-take is the art of coaching. The artistry comes in observing what they are able to do and using what you know to provide the environment and the tools for them to discover what more they can be. You are mentor, teacher, cheerleader and artist all rolled into one. The best thing is that your living creation keeps recreating itself in better and more surprising ways.

Because this is art, and art cannot be fully expressed on the printed page, I cannot tell you exactly how to do this with your particular team. You are in charge of the soccer; you know your kids. My purpose in this chapter is to give you a framework to assess their physical needs and a method to blend in the fitness. Because fitness needs and physical abilities vary considerably by age, the chapter is organized by age group. For each age group we'll begin with an on-the-field scenario that demonstrates a typical soccer shortcoming with an underlying physical component. Then I'll highlight the specific fitness that needs addressing and offer several age-appropriate fitness activities you can take directly into your practice sessions. Some will be standalone fitness games, but many will be activities meant to be part of the warm-up, skills training, field work or cool-down you're already doing. The chart at the end of the chapter summarizes all activities for all age groups, including video links you can take straight to the field.

Note that each recommended fitness activity uses physical skills necessary for the game, like running, jumping, leaping, landing, cutting, balancing, stopping and starting. Some involve the ball. All of them are referred to as "functional activities" because the whole body, not an isolated muscle, is trained while performing the activity. In this way, the activities are sport-specific as well as physical preparation, thus making efficient use of practice time. Be sure players know that the fitness portion of their training is as important as the technical portion. Performing it accurately and meticulously according to instructions on form and pace is critical for safety and effectiveness. Reinforce this by watching closely and keeping them on task. This is a great opportunity to observe and identify their weaknesses and imbalances, such as where one side or one muscle group is stronger or is favored, and to address the issues before they take a toll on their movement and their play.

I encourage you to join in. Most coaches can benefit from fitness, too, and participating may be the perfect opportunity to earn some respect or welcome some humility. Please don't send them off to "do fitness" while you set up the cones or talk to the assistant coach. They'll take it seriously only if you do.

Before you begin, be sure you know the standard physical, mental and emotional characteristics of the age group and gender you coach. I have included a brief listing in chapter 1. Best Practices for Coaches (http://www.vysa.com/docs/coaches/Best_Practices.pdf) is a terrific resource from the Virginia Youth Soccer Association website with a comprehensive outline for all ages, stages and abilities. Be sure your expectations for their fitness and your training fall well within the normal range for your group. Even so, if only a few of your players can successfully perform the fitness activity you initiate, revise the plan. Simplify it or reduce its intensity so they can be successful. Success motivates. It is also wise to have an assistant coach confirm that your instructions are clear and your demonstration is accurate. They can't do what they don't understand, no matter how many times you repeat it or how loudly.

Following is the general framework we'll use to take us from field to fitness to improved performance. If you're an experienced coach, you're probably already using a similar method for designing and planning technical and tactical training. Keep in mind that technical difficulties may partially be the result of physical shortfalls.

1. Watch team and individual play to identify what isn't working and what needs improvement.
2. Identify any physical issue preventing good performance of that skill.
3. Design the next practice plan with that theme in mind. Turn what isn't working into something that works better.
4. Add the fitness to this theme.
   - Start simple. Increase physical demands as soon as players can do so without compromising their form. This is the order for success: 1st accurate, 2nd strong, 3rd repeated, 4th at pace
   - Think "SAID": **S**pecific **A**pplication to **I**mposed **D**emands.
5. Then make it matter. Give them an objective or goal as a team or versus a teammate.
6. Make it fun. This can be competition or achievement for some. Or it may be silly—sing, clap, count, laugh. You left work at the office, right? They left it at school.
7. Finally, make it game-like, but watch for backsliding. We tend to default to what we're used to doing. Expect changes in form and fitness to be evident in play. If they

are missing, you may need to be more intentional in connecting fitness to form.

Let's use this as your typical practice outline. The letter in the parenthesis indicates where a game may fit in your practice plan.

- Warm-up (W)
- Physical activities to introduce theme—first without the ball, then with it (PA)
- Technical activities to apply the theme in combinations and small groups (T)
- Scrimmage or full-sided play to apply the theme to the game (G)
- Cool-down and debrief (C)

Here are the age group scenarios with fitness added. Feel free to hop to the age group of most interest to you. A chart summarizing the fitness games for each age group appears at the end of the chapter.

Initial Phase: U8

Game Scenario: The kids are excited to play their first game of the season. They kick off and take it down field, all the way into the opponent's goal box. Your strongest forward has it right in front of the goal. He winds up and…trips and falls…and the goalie scoops it up and clears it away.

Kids this age are still getting to know their bodies. Some are more coordinated than others, but their muscles and nerves and brain are still learning how to communicate with each other. They get ahead of themselves. Even if they know what they want to do, frequently they just can't do it. Fortunately, with time, growth and practice, these connections will be made and they will finish that shot. But in the meantime, you want to help them get to know their bodies. Maybe even speed this process. Help them learn what it feels like to execute movements, to keep their balance, to be dynamic. To be at home in their bodies.

Games: Athletes 8 and under love to have fun. They tend to be uninhibited and willing to try most anything. They will follow your directions and even make up a few of their own. Here are some games I use with my U8 athletes.

- **Crazy days** is a game for the whole team. Each player has a ball and must move with it in a defined space. They must follow your instructions about how to move, with what foot surface to control the ball or in what direction, avoiding teammates doing the same. You may impose a consequence for bumping, but make it fun (e.g., they have to apologize to their ball or pat it tenderly before they can continue). Don't exclude them. You might instruct them to stop on cue (visual/verbal or other) and/or execute the soccer skill you call out. Or they must leave the ball and hurdle, touch, squat on or otherwise interact with their own ball or a given number of other balls. This is good for warm-up or technical training. (W, T) (*Caution: younger ones may not want to leave "their" ball.*)

- **Crazy days in the zoo** is a modification of the basic version. Run your crazy days but call our (or have them call out) animals they must imitate in moving between the balls. Perhaps they will imitate the animal sounds, too. This looks and sounds silly, which makes it fun, but only you will know that gorilla walking teaches them how to lunge, laying eggs like hens teaches squat technique, and frog hopping teaches two-footed jumping, with bent knee landing improving knee safety. This is good for warm-up, physical training and cool-down. (W, PA, C)

- **Tag** is the forever favorite. Kids love to play it. They can organize it themselves, and it's very soccer-game-like. One player is "it" and the others run to avoid being tagged. Adaptations include freeze tag (frozen until you are tagged by a teammate) or TV tag (frozen only if you can't say a not-already-used TV show or movie before you are tagged) or stuck in the mud (frozen until a teammate crawls through your legs to free you). There are many versions of this game. You can also put conditions on it, such as having to hop or tag below the waist, or giving them bandana tails that must be snatched as a "tag." Let it be free play before practice and just put out some cones and pinnies. Tag provides a great cardiovascular workout, so have two taggers if some kids are just standing around. Tag requires coordinated body motion, change of direction, teamwork and field vision. And it's fun. Great for warm-up and cardio. (W, PA)

- Find ideas and rules for lots more kids' games at Games Kids Play (http://www.gameskidsplay.net).

Basic Phase: U9/U10

Game Scenario: Your players take the field. They are bouncing up and down with energy. They navigate deftly, using their skills. Your midfielder sees his target and winds up to send it forward. It gets about halfway there before the weak pass is intercepted. He runs forward to challenge for the ball, only to be denied with a body check that sends him to the ground. Hard.

Kids this age are starting to gain strength and coordination, but there is a big disparity from one kid to another. This is also the time they start noticing the differences among them—who is "good" and who is "not." Some who mature earlier may currently be good because they are bigger or faster. Time will often even up this disparity. Their bodies will do a lot of changing before they're grown, so it's important that they don't get a fixed idea of what they can do and what they can't. Help them focus on what they have to contribute now and encourage them to grow in other areas.

Get them to use their whole bodies, both left and right sides, in all directions. They are discovering what movement feels like, so get them moving. Now is the time to introduce proper stretching. Also, use their sense of play to engage teammates in ways that will help them grow, both physically and sportingly. Partner up kids of about the same size so they are not over-matched. Games that involve movement, change of direction, teamwork and physical challenge are perfect.

Most 9- and 10-year-olds are energetic until they're pooped. They may spend a lot of time in front of a screen when they are not at practice, so they may not be used to being outdoors in the heat or familiar with good old physical effort. Trick them. I like to play games that have an objective that stretches them to do a little more than they're used to "for the good of the team." Be sure to include plenty of water breaks, as kids can overdo it, and their small size makes heat a concern.

Here are some games I use with my 9- and 10-year-old athletes:

- **Obstacle course** takes some time to set up, depending on how detailed you want to be, but it gives you endless possibilities and keeps everyone moving. It can be as complicated as having stations where they have to execute particular moves or jumps or as simple as cones they have to hurdle, tip over, right or collect. I like to divide the team in half and have one group be the obstacles or gates for the other group. Then switch. You can encourage accuracy by having the gatekeeper count or motivate speed by timing the effort and pitting the first group against the second. Of course, do this at least twice to give team A the opportunity to beat Team B now that they know their honor is at stake. One of my favorites is "plank gates." Group A scatters and becomes the gates through which Team B must pass. They have to stay in plank position (tabletops!) as gates until all of Group B has finished. The drill has dual benefit since your gates are working core strength while your passers are working skill and stamina. For a little fun, allow the gates to "walk" or seal-crawl with laces on the ground and see how the passers problem-solve and accommodate the challenge.

Good for warm-up, technical and cardio fitness. (W, PA, T, G)

- **Shove the gamut** is a physical partner challenge. Set up a narrow channel of cones, then have kids pair off by size and line up with their partners at the mouth of the channel. They can interlock arms if they want, but they must stay in physical contact during the course of moving through the channel of cones. The object is for each kid to attempt to muscle his partner-opponent out of the course on his side. They may not extend an arm, pull or otherwise break soccer rules. Points are awarded to the team that fairly outmuscles his teammate in each pair. No points if they stay in the channel to its end. Either way it's great core strength and VERY game-like. I have also tried this with the objective being a ball rolled into the channel that must be won and controlled over the end line. (PA, G)

- **Relays** are always a hit. Be creative. Use a ball to execute maneuvers. Have them retrieve cones for their side. Have them start backwards, upside down, seated, with a somersault. Try a gradual build-up relay with teams of 3 or 4 with the first runner returning to "take" each teammate in turn so he/she runs alone on the first circuit, then with 2, 3 and 4, who then taps 2 to run, adding 3, 4 and 1 in turn and so on. (PA)

Basic Phase: U11/U12

Game Scenario: It's a 0–0 game, but your forwards have been banging away at the other team's goal all afternoon. You have dominated the possession and deserve the win. "Push up!" you yell to your defenders. They always tend to hang back, worried about the long ball over their heads, but you need their numbers to support your attack. But there's that one opposing striker with skills and moves and speed. She has the ball and nimbly navigates through 1, 2, 3 defenders. They are back on their heels as she heads for your goal with your players falling well behind. Your keeper is defenseless.

For kids this age everything is changing, on the inside and the outside. Nothing is simple anymore. They want to feel capable and in control, but that is fleeting. Growing bodies leave them less coordinated. And this is made worse by their awareness that people are watching them: their teammates, their parents and the boys (or girls) on the next field. The "more athletic" kids are emerging. The "less athletic" kids are sitting back. At 11 and 12, selection either by self or by culture starts to make its way. Kids start to dichotomize into the good and the not-good-enough. The not-good-enough go home.

It's commonly reported that by 12 years of age 70% of the kids who were playing at age 10 will drop out of sports. In my opinion, kids never reach a place where they are not good enough to play—and certainly not when they are 12. But our selection process often says so. If you coach a rec or less advanced travel team, you will have some of these players, perhaps many. You may have some players new to the game who are athletic but as yet unskilled with the ball. Your objective is to help all of them build confidence in their bodies. Soccer can be your means.

Even if you coach at the higher levels, you will have players who are a bit unfamiliar with the new bodies they are growing into. The demands of quicker play require agility and speed, coordination and balance. These are tough for them to manage when they've grown 3 inches over the summer and now totter on spindly legs. Some of your opponents may already be fielding the "early developing" kids who tower over their teammates and have beefed up like high school players. Agility will be your friend.

The size discrepancy brings with it another risk: injuries. At 11 and 12, kids are at the perfect age to build in dynamic training designed to balance, strengthen and reduce injuries. They are going to be adjusting to all the changes, so movement activities can help them get reacquainted. Find sample dynamic training routines that will work for your age group at: http://fit2finish. com/dynamic-warm-up-for-soccer-players/

Here are some games I use with my 11- and 12-year-olds to increase agility and reduce injury:

- **Agility course**, like the obstacle course, offers many options. Generally I set this up so the players have 8–10 quick repetitions of a particular movement; cones or balls placed relatively close together in a row form a simple course and require very little space. This also works well for pre-game when you don't have a warm-up field. I have them move through the course several times, the first using a simple maneuver to get warmed up (say, small steps forward), followed by increased challenge (moving sideways, slicing in and out, forward and backward). Help them be successful by requiring them to maintain focus through the whole course. Don't just tell them to focus, give them a focus cue, like *bellybutton facing* *me, let me see your smile, lead with your laces, stay on the balls of your feet, etc.* The repetitions will recruit muscle memory, and they will execute more naturally and more confidently. Key: insist on good form. This will require controlled speed as they learn to be accurate in the drill. An agility ladder is another option to use here. There are numerous online sites with demos of sample ladder drills. Or have your players come up with their own drills. First person in line determines the move, then the next, all the way through the line. (W, PA)

- **Expanded agility course** is useful because play requires quick change of direction, not only in tight spaces, but also on the move. Consider expanding your course to demand change of direction with bursts of speed in between. I want them to be safe as they pivot and/or reverse direction, so I cue them to sink low or bend their knees or be on the balls of their feet at these points. They must touch the cone or touch the heel of their outside foot at each cone. Or have them "slap 10" low to their teammate who is in squat position forming the gate as they go through forward, then back with a pivot in the middle. Alternative: add the ball and require moves/cuts, etc., at cones or within the course. (PA, G)

- **Reaction balls** are a fun playground or gym floor option to consider. They can be purchased at low cost from online fitness equipment suppliers. These small rubber balls have knobs all over their surface and produce an unpredictable bounce when dropped. Have a contest among partners, awarding points to the player who collects the ball on one hop or two or more bounces. Giggles will ring out, and you'll be amazed how quickly they defend their "collection space." (PA, G)

- Extra **home option**: Encourage them to run up the stairs when they get home, though warn the parents beforehand. It's funny how stadium step running is such drudgery for collegiate athletes, but younger kids get a kick out of "breaking the rules" at home. Parents, let 'em bound up the steps. Two at a time if they want. Great for plyometrics, power, agility and a bit of muscle endurance to boot. (PA)

Intermediate: U13/U14

Game Scenario: You beat this team last season 4-0, but they clearly have the edge today. Your players seem unsure on the ball. The few shots they take are off-target or weak, the players falling away as they shoot. Like the Leaning Tower of Pisa, they seem ready to tip even without assistance from the opponent. Even your few really strong players are wide of target or way over the top. Too bad they don't count 3 points for field goals in soccer. What is going on?

Kids this age are getting stronger. The more physically mature players are losing the lankiness and gaining some muscle. Others seem to have put all their growing into length and not breadth. You expected this. You just didn't expect it to look so inept on the soccer field. Coordination doesn't come right away with the new body type and dimensions. Skills that used to be simple must be "relearned" with the new kinesthetic sensation. It's like learning to play tennis with a child-sized racket and suddenly switching to the regulation length. It takes time to adjust.

Once they get it coordinated, kids revel in their new strength. They'll want to see how far or how hard or how high they can send it. Controlling this new power is another matter altogether. (And what good is a lead pass the opposing keeper collects every time?) Knowing this, insist that your players always have a target both for direction and distance. Ask, *What are you aiming at? What is the weight of the ball sent?* The soccer reason for this is obvious: you hit your target much more often when you have one. The physical reason is this: they must learn to control their new strength to make it work for them. Or as Yoda said to Luke, "With great power comes great responsibility."

The goal here is a "balance of power"—muscles working together, not one muscle or muscle group that dominates or overpowers the others. Physiologically, it is designed to work this way. The muscle force exerted by the contracting muscles starts the motion, while the opposing muscles gradually activate eccentrically (contract as they lengthen) to control and slow the motion. This is why the follow-through is so important to execution of the skill and why a sudden, unanticipated stop can cause injury. The "start" and the "stop" of the motion must be choreographed to protect the joint. This is a neuromuscular phenomenon. The information flow is essential from brain to muscle and back to brain again to communicate balance and coordination information.

To train this I advocate what I call the North-South-East-West approach to balanced strengthening, especially with this age group. Drills are designed to strengthen dynamically on all sides of the active joints. For soccer players this gives extra time to the "opposing and supporting" muscles that aren't the prime force generators in most movements. Functional strengthening of muscles like the outer thigh (abductors), the hamstrings and the anterior lower leg muscles is essential. In the normal run of play, they may be overlooked, while quads, inner thighs, calves and Achilles are worked to exhaustion. Exhausted muscles then default to weaker ones or give way, and the result may be disaster. This form of overtraining is common in athletes who execute the same motions over and over, and leaves them ripe for injury.

That's the other thing you hear from this group: something always hurts. But beware of writing these off as "just growing pains." Areas of rapid growth, like growth plates, are especially fragile. In active kids we compound the insult with the constant tugging of active muscles at these sites. This results in inflammation, pain and injury. Be aware of this. It's not "just a growing pain"; it's an overuse injury requiring ice and rest. Don't make a nagging soreness into a full-blown injury. Keep these injuries at bay by stretching and strengthening in the "danger zones" if they can do this without pain. Stretching allows the muscles to lengthen and catch up with growing bones, and, along with gentle increases in muscle use and tension, will prepare the bony attachments to withstand the demands. Be patient with these athletes.

Here are some games I use with my 13- and 14-year-olds to increase functional, dynamic strength and balance and reduce the potential for injury.

- **Leap and hold** requires a zigzag course of small flat cones at a distance just a bit further than they can leap off of one foot. For the first run-through, instruct them to stand facing forward and leap diagonally toward each cone, hold for 2 full counts and then leap to the next cone. Landings should be stable with foot directed straight ahead (absorb lateral landing force with bent-knee balance) and "as low as they can go." Staying low helps with stability and gives them the powerful position to take off to the next cone. Keep them honest by positioning yourself at the end of the cone course and stopping them at random with a visual signal. This forces them to keep their heads up, which helps with balance. It is also fun to have 2 or 3 lines leaping at once, leaving less time standing and more time to try it. Coaching Cue: most kids have a weaker side. Choose this for your hands-up stop so they are made to stabilize there. (T, PA)

- **Partner 2-legged pushes** improves dynamic core strength. Have Player 1 lie on the ground with both legs extended upward, knees straight, ankles flexed and locked. Instruct them to keep legs straight and together. Player 2 stands at his partner's head, one foot on either side of partner's ears, toes facing the lifted legs. Player 1 (lying) grabs hold of Player 2's ankles for support. The object is for Player 2 to push Player 1's feet down or to either side and for Player 1 to resist the push. Start with easy pushes in a given direction, then increase pressure and mix up the direction. Then switch partner positions. As coach, watch that knees don't bend; this can be challenging for players with poor hamstring flexibility. Excellent core and torso strengthening and very fun. (PA, C)

- **Resistance band tag** is a fast and fun game made appropriate for all ages by varying the weight of the band resistance. Each player is issued an elastic band 3–4 feet in length. (Purchase bands or rolls of bands at sporting goods stores or online fitness supply sites.) For this age group, use moderately heavy bands (levels 2 or 3). They come in at least 4 resistance levels, so gauge the strength of your team before you choose. Have them tie the band in a taut loop around their legs while they stand with feet together. Bands may then be positioned 3/4 of the way up the shin guards (harder) or around thighs (easier). To move in bands, they may hop, jump or run in small steps, but they should accomplish this without letting the bands fall down or pulling their knees inward. They must "keep the rectangle" made by their shins, the ground and the stretched band. I cue them "no triangles," which means no rolling in of the knees. Then, assign one or two players to begin as taggers. Without bands, they must dribble within a prescribed area, attempting to tag their teammates by passing (not driving) the ball into them. You are tagged if the ball hits you below the knees. Teammates move to elude being tagged and may jump repeatedly to avoid close challenges. Once you are tagged, you slide off your band and become a tagger. Last one left is first tagger next game. Great plyometrics, outer thigh strengthening and endurance plus bonus ball-handling skills. (W, PA, T, G)

- **Developmental flexibility** requires designing a static stretching routine for *after* every practice and every game, with dynamic stretching *before*. The players should know it and be able to execute it with perfect form and serious intent. (See chapter 5 for details and pictures.) Not only stretching for recovery, but stretching to develop flexibility and maintain range of motion, is a must for this age group. This is because their growth in height will leave many, perhaps most, with decreased flexibility, especially the boys. Tightness invites injury. (C)

- **Injury prevention** special note: As these kids get stronger, move and stop more quickly and experience stronger physical challenges on the field, they are more subject to injury. The 13- and 14-year-old age group must have injury prevention drills and activities planned into their training routine as preparation for the demands of the game. Injury prevention focus for boys is dynamic strength, power and agility to absorb and avoid collisions. For girls it's balanced strength, dynamic agility and plyometric movement recruiting hamstrings (sink low and spring up) to make their jumping, landing and change of direction safer. (See chapter 7 for the details of common injuries and their prevention.)

Advanced: U15–U18

Game Scenario: Twelve players are all you can field today. Two are injured, three are at mandatory school events, one is playing for her AAU basketball team in a tournament this weekend. They start strong, and you are a goal up at halftime. But they amble into the halftime huddle rubbing their ankles, massaging their knees. Second half they battle, but they're tired. They are late to the ball and are the losers in collisions.

Kids this age are tired. Not yet adults, they are told they can do it all and they try. Even strong, skilled, capable players bend under the weight of the schedules they keep, the demands they face and the expectations they have for themselves. The best thing we can teach these kids is to respect the body they have been given. Train it well and treat it right and it will respond. Abuse it with poor eating, lack of sleep, stress and overdoing, and it will balk. Nothing responds well to abuse. Too often our kids embrace martyrdom—do it if it kills me—ignoring the consequences. Teens may feel invincible, but as adults, we know differently. We need to inject this foresight into the kids we coach.

If you're low on subs, particularly on a hot day, be aware of the stress that playing minutes place on your players. Substitute high energy-expending positions as much as you can. Be aware, too, of the condition of the kids coming into the game. Be sure they are well hydrated (more about this in chapter 6, Fueling the Athlete for Performance). Some may be rushing from another event or another competition. That's great dedication, but it takes a toll physically. As you see them losing steam, coach them to be wise in their play. It may even go against your normal 100% effort, 100% of the time. Knowing when to conserve is key. Advise them not to sprint after balls they won't save and to be smart about how and when to tackle. Is a win today really worth losing a player to injury for 4–6 weeks or longer?

Relationships are key with all of our players, but particularly so as they grow into young men and women. As their coach, you are a valuable member of their life team. They may share things with you that they'll tell no one else. Win their trust by earning it. Be available, honest and confidential when requested. Find out what's going on in their lives. A demanding lifestyle saps their energy just as much as a series of sprints, but they may not be expecting it. Be aware of the state of their mind as well as the state of their body. They need you to care, not just about their soccer but about them. Want what's best, and they'll give it to you.

So how do we prepare them and ourselves for the high school level game? Here are 5 categories of physical and fitness strategies.

- Help them become aerobically fit with the least impact on their body. I highly recommend the interval training approach for aerobic and anaerobic fitness training in this age group. Shorter bursts of high intensity effort give you maximum fitness in minimum time. However, endurance for the whole game, or for their lives on fast forward, requires longer intervals with shorter rest periods. Gradually build in repetitions and reduce rest. Use the game, an expanded field size, multiple balls in play and team cooperation to keep it fun. (PA, G)

- Remember the skills, and call on finesse over force. Stronger kids, especially as they tire, can be tempted to use brawn over dexterity. It takes less energy to run you over than to win the ball from you fairly. They come running in with no intention of stopping, even if the other player doesn't move. This is a recipe for injury, to them or their opponent. Even if the ref doesn't whistle this kind of play, refrain from coaching it, rewarding it or encouraging it. Field skilled, fit players. They will need those bodies for a long time.

- Pay attention when kids report niggles (those irritating sorenesses, aches and twinges) and become knowledgeable about what should and what shouldn't be played through, what needs stretching, rest, strengthening, etc. (see chapter 7 for more). Know when to recommend that a health professional take a look. Teach them to monitor their own bodies, and encourage them to be honest in reporting to you. Assure them that they won't be penalized in play if they need time off and that you'll do everything you can to keep them playing if their soreness is not serious. Early in the season and with players overlapping on other teams, be particularly attuned to the niggles.

- Cross-training is essential for this age group. Rotating the fitness and playing activities in your practices helps give them days of rest without "taking days off." Also, communicating with players and, where possible, with their other coach helps you plan an appropriate schedule for individual players.

- Prioritize your own activities and help your players prioritize theirs. No one can do it all. Don't expect that they can. If they are playing for multiple teams or participating in more than one sport in a season and this is impairing their performance, talk to them about choosing one team as the priority in each season. Let them see how you prioritize your life schedule and your coaching. Share with them how you select which training items to tackle and at what intensity, depending on whether you are in season or out, near game day or mid-week. Fitness improves only when the body can comply with demands, and it does so gradually.

The games I play with U13s and U14s I also play with high schoolers, but I use the ball and the game to greater advantage:

- **Resistance band tag** takes on a new vengeance. Use larger spaces and advise the taggers to "make the band-wearers work" before they tag them. Insist they pass into and not shoot at teammates! (W, PA, T, G)
- **Hop and volley** trains agility and outer thigh dynamic strength. Form partner pairs and have each pair set up 3 tall cones close together in a straight line. Player 1 (the volleyer) starts by standing sideways to the line of cones and leaps over and back in rhythm, leading with one foot and matching feet on the other side before bounding back. Partner 2 (the tosser) stands in front of the cones and feeds easy, accurate ball tosses, first to one side and then the other, leading the player over the cones. Player 1 volleys the ball with the laces back into the tosser's hands each time. Make it competitive by counting how many accurate volleys they complete in 30 seconds or 1 minute. Then switch tosser and volleyer. (PA, T, G)
- **V-passing** trains quickness, safe change of direction, receipt of pass and touch. Set up 3 tall cones in a triangle about 3–4 yards apart in a V shape pointing "away" from player 1 with the ball. Player 2 starts at the point of the V and runs to the outside of one cone, receives a rolled or passed ball from his partner, one-touches it back,

then straddles and hand touches the middle (point) cone before sprinting to the outside of the other cone. There he receives the pass, one-touching and sprinting back to the middle to touch and run to receive the pass on the opposite side. Counting passes completed in a limited time can make this competitive. As coach, watch to be sure players sink their hips to touch the middle cone for a quick pivot rather than "lazily" bending from the waist, which rounds the turn and ruins the "V." (It's a V, not a U!) The larger the separation between V-cones, the more fitness is demanded in this drill. (PA, T, G)

- **Fitness on their own** expects motivated high school athletes to train on their own or in pick-up fitness activities with their teammates. A schedule of fitness expectations, such as the mile run at a 7-minute pace, or # repetitions of full field "doggies," out and back to each of the field lines in a prescribed time, can provide motivation for making the team standard.

Fitness Games

U8 goal: Coordination, body awareness

Crazy days warm-up: https://www.youtube.com/watch?v=o42FawclTEc

Crazy days in the zoo: https://www.youtube.com/watch?v=59SjtO3gA9Q

U10 goal: Bi-lateral strength, body movement, speed

Obstacle course: https://www.youtube.com/watch?v=tf678sxNFwo

Shove the gamut: https://www.youtube.com/watch?v=WLc6Fy_lUOE

U12 goal: Body control, agility, reaction time

Basic agility course: https://www.youtube.com/watch?v=NLo6eY081ys

Expanded agility course: https://www.youtube.com/watch?v=y6uSW1suid0

U14 goal: Dynamic strength, balance, injury prevention

Leap and hold:
https://www.youtube.com/watch?v=FCT5u-3hPAg

Partner 2-legged pushes: https://www.youtube.com/watch?v=Jpa4kLJsOX4

Resistance band tag: https://www.youtube.com/watch?v=5kFruwvPPz8

U18 goal: Endurance, smart play, relationships

Hop and volley: https://www.youtube.com/watch?v=zed9GXhQDvo

V-passing:
https://www.youtube.com/watch?v=K0o8eqFtIgc

5

Flexibility, Stretching and Recovery

F lexibility is considered a critical element of overall body fitness, but is it really that important for sports performance? After all, there's not enough time to do everything, and kids' bodies are generally pretty flexible. Do we really need stretching? Yes. It's an important part of pre-game preparation, post-game recovery and regeneration between games.

While soccer players don't need the extreme flexibility that gymnasts and figure skaters require, they need a generous range of motion around their most-used joints to accomplish the skills of the game. (Note: Goalkeepers require attention to additional joints and more extensive flexibility training.) If you've seen a field player reach high with a leg to block a chest high cross or trap a wayward pass, you've witnessed this. Players who contort their bodies to execute a bicycle kick or bend high over a defender to deflect a header toward goal are even more extreme examples. Even running, stopping and changing direction suddenly at a sharp body angle requires flexibility. They need to be able to move freely and smoothly at all their joints, to bend and not break.

We think of kids as resilient; they spring back. They do tend to be limber and agile, especially compared to their coaches, perhaps. Their young bodies do provide for a lot of give and take, elasticity in all of the body's tissues. But today's soccer athletes have two things working against them that we must note but don't want to change: they're growing and they're active.

Growing kids have quickly changing body proportions, as we discussed in chapter 2. Lengthening limbs have taut muscles that beg for some stretching. Regular activity adds increased tone, even to resting muscles, in proportion to their use. They are wound tight. This puts their longer limbs in a precarious position. Ideally, if their activity recruited all of their muscles equally, they'd have balanced strength and motion around each joint, but this, of course, is not the case. Their gangly build and often awkward coordination tells you this. Their increase in length and then breadth seems to happen almost at random.

On top of this we add training. They favor their dominant side and choose preferred movements. Right footers send ball after ball to the left side with the right instep. The left leg extends as support. The same muscles tug their joints from one side or in one direction while resting muscles stand by and watch. Imbalances grow. Movement becomes inefficient and lacks the smooth flow that spells healthy, natural flow. Instead of stronger, faster, balanced players, we get kids complaining of aches and pains, subject to strains or, worse, muscle pulls or tears. Kids need to stretch.

Sport science says:

- *Dynamic stretching before activity* prepares the muscles, joints and neuromuscular connections
- *Static stretching after activity* reestablishes hard-working muscles to resting lengths, an important part of recovery
- *Ballistic stretching* should be done rarely or not at all
- *Regular stretching that becomes routine* develops flexibility and addresses the tightness that comes with play and a healthy, growing body

Sound complicated? It's not. Here we go. First, some definitions:

- Dynamic stretching: lengthening of the muscles as the body moves through the normal range of motion around a joint or joints
- Static stretching: lengthening of the muscles in a static, stilled or holding position
- Ballistic stretching: quick lengthening stretch of a muscle using a bouncing, ballistic or explosive motion

Let's break it down to the three opportunities coaches have to include flexibility training in their athletes' workouts: pre-activity, post-activity and between sessions.

Pre-activity

Preparing the body for activity with a general warm-up for the whole body followed by active dynamic stretching of a sport-specific nature is best. General warm-up with walking, jogging or skipping increases the temperature and blood flow to the working muscles and joints, preparing them for movement. Then comes active dynamic warm-up, by accentuated "rehearsing" of the kinds of movements that will be demanded, activating the neuromuscular connections and calling on familiar motor patterns to coordinate movement.

The dynamic warm-up follows a pattern. Establish a pre-practice dynamic routine that starts with slower, lower intensity movement using smaller or fewer muscle groups and then progressively increases in intensity. Encourage players to use their whole range of motion in all movement planes: forward, backward, sideways, diagonal and with rotation. Instruct and then insist on proper form. End with short sprints or changes of pace that simulate game effort. This should prepare players to transition immediately to the physical demands of the game.

Here is a sample dynamic warm-up with 18 paired steps. If you're on a lined field, the 18-yard box provides a perfect setup. If not, step off 15-18 yards and mark with cones. Remember to emphasize good form; this is not designed to be fitness work. Emphasize bent knees and staying on the balls of the feet to make it an injury prevention warm-up, too.

Beginner/basic:

focus is learning the correct movement and taking time to get it right

- Jog forward
- Jog backward
- Walk on heel-heel, toe-toe
- Little ankle kicks/flicks
- Slide side (facing right, moving left); NO clicking of heels together
- Slide side (facing right, moving right)
- Slide forward, alternating right and left diagonal ("Wizard of Oz")
- Drop step (backward "Wizard of Oz")
- Knee up and out, "open the gate" (do as 3-count: step-step-knee up and out; this results in alternating legs)
- Knee out, in and down, "close the gate"
- Carioca left with emphasis on first step across (1—2-3-4 and repeat)
- Carioca right (1—2-3-4)
- Step kick to opposite hand (do as 3-count as above; keep body upright: foot lifted to touch suspended hand)
- Step and "T"-lean (balanced on one leg, the other extended straight behind with toe down, arms out to the sides in a T)
- High knees
- Butt kicks
- Sprint to quick, multi-step stop (out)
- Sprint to quick, multi-step stop (back)

Intermediate/advanced:

focus is game preparation along with proper technique

Perform the dynamic warm-up outlined above for joint mobilization (see the Fit2Finish video demonstration at https:// www.youtube.com/watch?v=Fu5MiL1XHN8). Then add some strength and balance builders. For core strength, use planks; for leg strength, lunges or Russian hamstrings; for balance, 1-legged stance with partner challenge; for power, plyometrics; and for agility, plant and cut drills. All of these can be modified in intensity for various ages and abilities. The FIFA 11+ program offers their version with demos by Alex Morgan and Cobi Jones here: http://www.youtube.com/playlist?list=PL-W9Gn-XDQ_ pIeE4mo1mgBb4OwyGc0UGU.

Then move on to warm-ups with the ball. You may want to intersperse some "quick check" stretching with your ball warm-up. Teach your players a systematic routine to "quick check" for any tightness they might be feeling by stretching and holding for 2-3 seconds at each of the major joints. Have them perform in right and left pairs so they can compare bilateral flexibility. Athletes can always tell you which side is tighter, and this tunes them in and tunes them up. Active Isolated Stretching, made popular by Jim and Phil Wharton, is based on similar principles.[2]

Sport science today is clear that players should *not* perform sustained, static stretches during pre-game warm-up. These can be damaging to cold muscles and detrimental to the power and quickness necessary for sports performance. Still, I see many "old

---

2   Active Isolated Stretching is a dynamic stretching technique of short duration which avoids triggering the stretch reflex. See http://www. stretchingusa.com/active-isolated-stretching.

school" coaches doing them. Don't be one of them. It is safe to use these brief stationary "quick check" stretches as an effective way to single out injury-prone tightness for extra care and tending. Experienced players can use these as a "physical checklist" to identify what feels tight. Tightness signals a muscle that needs a bit more dynamic attention and should be a focus for post-activity sustained, developmental stretching.

Here is a sample checklist of muscles and movements that can be used for the "quick check."

- Hip flexor—front of thigh at hip (upper quad) *keep abdominals tight to stabilize pelvis
- Hip extensor—back of thigh at hip (upper hamstring)
- Hip abductor—outer thigh
- Hip adductor—inner thigh
- Quadriceps—front of thigh at knee
- Hamstring—back of thigh at knee
- Calf/Achilles—back of ankle/heel *be sure heel and toe are aligned
- Shin/tibialis—front of ankle, laces down
- Ankle circles—toe points down, ankle is rotated smoothly
- For more advanced players add gluteal, lower back, upper back, shoulders, and triceps.
- For goalkeepers add arms, shoulders, hands and torso (see below).

Here is a sample goalkeeper dynamic warm-up routine:

- Rolling figure 8—in a wide stance, roll ball between the legs and around the outside of each, tracing a figure 8

- Bend knee in a sideward lunge on the side where ball is rolled
- Standing torso twists
- Standing torso bends, right and left
- Arm circles—large motion, individually and then together, forward and backward
- Arms over head, down and behind—can include ball bounce in this
- Quick sets of multi jumps off two feet, bringing knees to chest in tuck jump (more advanced)
- Jumps to (aim to) touch bar with each hand
- Wrist circles R and L
- Bend fingers gently back toward forearm
- Bend fingers together down toward ground (best if arm is extended at elbow to do this)

Post-activity: postgame recovery

Now is the time for the static stretching; don't skip it. These static stretches will begin to return players' hard-worked muscles back to their resting lengths and their joints to balanced positioning. If there is one opportunity most coaches miss to enhance the health and fitness of their players, it is this one. And it really adds no extra time at all. You're probably already huddling them for a post-game chat (or post-practice info session). Have them stretch while you say what you need to say. Create a regular routine of stretches for them to go through post-game or post-practice.

Follow these important guidelines when instructing the static stretches.

- Hold each stretch just at the point of tension, not pain, for at least 20–30 seconds. Do not overstretch. Ballistic (bouncing) stretches and overstretching activate the "stretch reflex," which contracts the muscle you are trying to stretch and negates the stretch.

- Stretch along the line of muscle pull from its origin to insertion. Because multiple muscles may attach at slightly different sites near the joint, a simple change in orientation can change the effectiveness of a stretch. Beware of favoring a more elastic tendon over its taut counterpart. Know the correct form. Teach it to your players and insist that they do it correctly. Major offenders are the quad stretch done with knee tugged sideways rather than straight back and the Achilles stretch done with toe pointed outward rather than straight forward.

- Make sure your athletes understand that stretching is an important part of training for performance, recovery and injury prevention.

- There's no single correct set of stretches, but include the muscles/body parts most used just as you do for warm-up. You can have your athletes experiment with what position works best for them (standing, sitting, kneeling, lying). Be flexible. Field or weather conditions (like a wet or muddy field) may demand one over another.

- As the coach, you will need to teach and then lead stretches for younger players. But train your team leaders in the routine so they can begin leading it with their teammates. When kids begin leading, be sure to watch and make sure they are covering all the important joints and holding the stretches for the necessary length of time. Caution: kids will announce the stretch, do it and start counting before teammates have even gotten into position. They will also count seconds at lightning speed. Teach them to be observers and to be patient with their teammates. Hurried stretches done wrong are time wasted.

Soccer stretches for coaches and athletes

These stretches will take just a few minutes after each practice and game, but this is time well spent. One coach contacted me to say his biggest challenge is parents who want to whisk their kids away. Yes, we are in a hurry these days. Just email those team parents and let them know you are planning to stretch. This is an important part of the training. Then welcome them to join you.

Here, in images, are stretches for the field. Remember to hold static stretches for 20–30 seconds to develop flexibility and fully stretch muscles that have been worked.

Hip flexor stretch: Be sure front knee goes no further than the big toe.

Hamstring stretch: Hip is pushed back, leg fully extended, toe up. Be sure both hips are "square" (i.e., you're not leaning in).

Quadriceps stretch: Hips square, abdominals tight, heel pulled toward glutes. Some like to hold their hand in the air or put a finger on the belly button to remind the core to stay strong.

Quadriceps stretch (side-lying option): Support leg is slightly bent for balance. Keep torso straight and tummy tight. This fixes the pelvis in place to isolate and anchor the stretch.

Achilles/calf stretch: Be sure heel is pushed down to the ground and toe is pointed straight ahead. If heel cannot reach the ground, walk feet in and bend more at the waist.

Anterior shin stretch: Toe drags. Push laces toward the ground.

Inner thigh stretch: Use elbows to push thighs away for extra stretch.

Inner thigh stretch (alternative): Hands push from behind to intensify stretch. Added benefit: hamstring and calf can be stretched from this position.

Outer hip/piriformis stretch: I call this the "figure 4" stretch. Elbow pushes crossed knee away while extended leg is pulled in. Be sure hips are square.

Hamstring sit and reach stretch: Reach and hold toes to provide the best hamstring stretch. Can do one leg at a time or use a towel or band to pull.

Age group hints for effective stretching with your team:

- Youngest kids are just learning what their bodies feel like. Be patient. Make it fun to feel.
- Elementary kids like to do it as a group. With my girls I did a "daisy circle." Boys did spokes of a motorcycle. Circle it up so they can see you and you can see and chat with them. Be sure you demonstrate properly AND show correct form. Most won't be able to reproduce what they see immediately. Have assistants circulate to help them feel the right position.
- Older elementary kids know the routine and can be led through stretches by the team leader or captain. Check in with them, though, or they will just choose their favorites and/or rush through, negating the value of the stretching.
- Middle school and high school kids who have been playing for a while know their bodies. They will tell you which muscles are tight and which leg is less flexible. Give them the responsibility of working on the "bad" leg, after practice and at home, but don't assume they will. Insist on it after practice and regularly check to be sure that they are maintaining good form.
- Coaches, you need to stretch, too! Stretching with your players is a great way to model your investment in the value of flexibility training. Plus, most of us are not very active during the day. Sitting leaves muscles tight and joints stiff. Our bodies are not as elastic and supple as they used to be. Am I wrong? Stretching will do you good.

I hear coaches dismiss their teams calling out, "Be sure and stretch when you get home!" As if that'll ever get done. They skip stretching on the field, maybe thinking that something so easy can't possibly be worth the time. They figure that time on the field should be *work*ing out. We know, though, that the body must recover from hard effort. Otherwise any training they've done suffers. Flexibility is the part of training designed to help them bounce back. Think of it as dessert at the end of the meal. They've earned it.

Home Program: Players will develop their flexibility, enhance range of motion, and reduce soreness and injury risk by performing their stretches all days of the week, not just at practice and on game days. Encourage this. Suggest that they stretch when they have been somewhat active but not first thing in the morning or last thing before bed, if possible. Here is a basic stretching routine that hits all the major muscle groups for soccer coaches and athletes: http://fit2finish.com/soccer-stretches-for-coaches-and-athletes/.

Stretching Equipment: I believe simple equipment, creatively used, is the most efficient and cost- effective way to bring training to the field. Plus, it is accessible to most every coach and player. I use resistive elastic bands for field fitness training and stretching. I also recommend using a simple 6–8 foot rope, which you can purchase for very low cost at your local home supply store, to assist in some stretches. See a sample stretching program that makes use of the rope for some stretches at http://fit2finish.com/stretches-for-athletes-who-run/.

Foam rollers have become very popular for home exercise, stretching and self-massage. I love them. You can purchase them online or from local sporting goods stores at relatively low cost. They come in a variety of densities. The more compressible ones are gentler but less resilient and become deformed after relatively short-term use and storage. I use and recommend the denser (often black) variety for youth athletes.

To use them, simply balance the body part of concern on top of the foam and, keeping your core tight, roll your body along the foam roller, allowing it to press into the aggravated area(s). Rolling has a bit of a learning curve because you must balance your body as you roll. This makes it into a functional exercise as well as a stretch-massage. Maximum effectiveness comes from a regular rolling routine, daily or multiple times in a day. The intensity of the applied pressure can be controlled by increasing or decreasing the surface area exposed to the roller. Point-pressing one area focuses intensity; distributing pressure over a larger area diminishes intensity.

Note: Foam rollers, even when used properly on very tight muscles, may be uncomfortable. Massaging out the areas of tension, compressing areas of inflammation and breaking up adhesions after an injury all involve discomfort in the rolling. This will diminish with regular use. As a bonus, foam rollers allow easy right-to-left comparison for areas of tightness.

Between sessions: rest and recovery from activity

Rest for recovery may be the best kept secret in the winning coach's arsenal. We don't "see" the repair, recovery and rejuvenation, and we're likely to attribute the gains only to the hard work in training. But we see the consequences when we forget or forgo the time for recovery; fatigue, burnout and injury top the list. When well applied, decreases in training load and time off from competition and play allow recovery in all facets of an athlete's life. And we know that many of our high school students, and increasingly our middle school kids, are under a great deal of stress socially, mentally, psychologically and physically. A good coach is keen to watch players individually for signs of overdoing it.

Given those complexities, managing the physical recovery may be the easiest of all. For the athlete to succeed, it is absolutely essential. For younger and recreational-level players, recovery comes in the form of plentiful water breaks, halftime oranges and a flexibility focus after practice sessions and games. Parents of these players are generally interested in nutrition information to support their active kids' needs, so be prepared to supply suggestions (see next chapter). For some, maintaining a healthy weight is a concern.

For travel, select or club level players, a wise coach plans rest and recovery days into the training schedule. You may be saying, whoa! What about those other teams? If they're training when we aren't, won't they get ahead? Not if you're smart and apply the sport science. This "keep up with the Joneses" mentality is rampant in our parenting and our youth sports today, but it is fear-based and not supported by science.

The science says:

- Growth hormone secretions peak at the onset of deep sleep. Be sure they get enough sleep. Lack of sleep has also been indicted in poor weight control.
- Rest offers the time for rebuilding. The body can redirect energy resources to "non-urgent" body regions instead

of the highly stressed areas that demand it the rest of the time.

- Properly applied training load is a stressor. Remodeling and repair require rest and recovery for adaptation. The new tissue is stronger and able to withstand a slightly greater stress. This is the cycle of healthy growth and the means to improve physical performance and achieve competitive success.

- Over-large training load or insufficient recovery time disrupts the cycle and may disable it. Many would say that "over-training" is really only "under-rest."

- Planned, realistic progression is the key to effective training. Young bodies are built block by block, and today's work is layered on yesterday's foundation. We must take care to stretch their minds and bodies to do all they can do.

To learn more about using recovery as a training tool, see http://fit2finish.com/work-and-recovery-are-essential-to-high-performanceinterval-training-is-most-gamelike/. And if you're wondering how much soccer is too much to be healthy for your kid, see http://fit2finish.com/everybody-wants-a-piece-of-my-kid-calculate-dont-negotiate/.

So schedule your rest and recovery right into your team schedule. When you put your tournaments on the calendar and ink in your practice days, stamp your R&R days after hard efforts, game days and after travel. Even if you want to meet the team after a week full of games, have it be a recovery day to get the kinks out and attend to the niggles. Please don't be the coach that runs them for 90 minutes because their game performance was dismal. You're defeating your purpose and putting your athletes at risk.

With advanced high school, college and pro players, planning the schedule for training, competition and rest is more complex. These players train most days of the week and will be targeting portions of the season for peak fitness. Coaches do well to employ periodization training with these athletes. Generally, there are two 2–3 month blocks, probably Sept-Oct-Nov and March-April-May, for peak match performance. More intense fitness conditioning can be safely performed pre-season and recovery time planned during the winter break and the summer break. Trends in the United States are toward "there's no such thing as a pre-season" because we're always in season. This needs to change if we want to keep our athletes healthy and progressing in their training.

A sample competitive team period plan might look like this:

- July-Aug—higher volume fitness
- *Sept-Oct-Nov—decreases in conditioning with increased intensity in play
- Dec-Jan-Feb—intensity decreases; gradual reconditioning with higher volume demands
- *Mar-Apr-May—similar to fall
- June—break

*In season, general conditioning declines and sport-specific conditioning as part of the game is favored.

It serves us well to remember the wisdom behind the interval training model here. Periodization is really just a larger application of this. A bout of intense demand followed by rest allows the body to perform at a higher level in the next training bout. This series of intervals—work: rest: work: rest—allows the body to work harder with less risk of injury. It is the same for the larger scheme of training. Peak play followed by full rest brings players back stronger, more focused and hungry to play well.

Let's not miss that opportunity. Coaches, give them time off to be kids. Their brains and their bodies work best when they have a chance to rest and recover. Don't let your team parents talk you into more training, one more tournament or a team sleepover before the big game! Help your players put their best cleat forward; then be satisfied with a job well done.

Trust your instincts. Don't give in to the Joneses. They don't know the sport or the science. You're the expert.

6

Fueling the Athlete
for Performance

A body performs best with high-quality nutrition, just as an engine purrs on high-test fuel. Feeding today's athlete on today's schedules can be a challenge. The goal should be sufficient calories taken throughout the day from a variety of healthy sources that include recommended levels of vitamins and minerals. Special preparation must be made for the particularly challenging game days and multi-game tournament days. Coaches and parents must be diligent in watching kids for unhealthy eating patterns and creative with kids who have special nutritional needs. Later in this chapter we'll discuss disordered eating and special populations.

Trends in American eating

It seems as if everyone out there has a new diet book or nutrition plan. We are a nation obsessed with what we eat, but as far as I can tell, this is doing nothing to help us maintain a healthy weight. The US Centers for Disease Control and Prevention concluded from the National Health and Nutrition Examination Survey (NHANES 2009–10) that 68 percent of US adults and approximately 1/3 of our children are overweight or obese. Many of today's adults didn't grow up in an environment that helped them develop healthy eating habits, and now as we get more sedentary, we are paying for that. Our children shouldn't.

When it comes to nutrition and young people, advising them to eat right so they won't get heart disease or diabetes falls on deaf ears. For those who already have started down the road toward overweight and obesity, these admonitions fall on ashamed ears. They are already very aware of how their jeans fit and that everyone is looking at them, so there's no point in berating them and adding to their shame. How do we get their attention to turn this thing around? Eating well for sports performance is a terrific venue for this conversation. We need to divert from "you're overweight" or "you're a beanpole" to "quality in, quality out." For active kids interested in sports like soccer, dangle the carrot of performance. Tell them, "If you want to play well for all 60 or 90 minutes, you need to fuel up on what will get you there." This chapter will show you (and them) what will get them there.

The science of nutrition is a huge field of study that is constantly scrutinizing how we eat. Nutrition is complicated, and it seems that recommendations keep changing. This inconsistent guidance has been a source of frustration for many "dieters" in

America who have pretty much thrown up their hands in defeat. Good science mixed with marketing hype, human guilt and fear have stirred up a multi-billion dollar industry in diet products, self-help books and group programs. But "diet" shouldn't be a 4-letter word. Diet is simply what you eat: the nutrients your body has available for energy to burn and to build and repair itself. Our challenges revolve around quantity, quality and convenience. We need properly portioned food from a healthy source and we don't want to wait. This takes planning and preparation and a little bit of nutrition know-how.

Nutrition know-how

We're always burning a few calories; the more active we are, the more calories we burn. At rest, most of the calories we burn come from fat, but, alas, we don't burn many. Through light exercise like walking, we split our recruitment, half from carbohydrate stores in the muscle and liver and half from fat storage. As we increase the intensity of exercise, our bodies prefer to utilize carbohydrates over fat because glycogen (the storage form of carbohydrates) is easier for the body to access than stored fat. Fat is a better storage depot for calories but is stubborn. That's why athletes performing at moderate to high intensities on the field call on ready-carbs (blood sugars), stored carbs (in muscle and liver) and some fats. The percentage of energy from fats will increase after about 60 minutes of activity, as glycogen supplies start to diminish. This shift to a greater percentage of fat utilization is thought to occur somewhat sooner in well trained athletes, allowing them to perform at optimum intensity longer.

In a nutshell, that's the energetics in the properly fed athlete. It should make this obvious: bodies don't perform well when they are running on empty. If glycogen stores get significantly depleted and if athletes don't replenish sufficiently between games or over the course of multiple practices, blood sugar can get dangerously low. Performance suffers. If they "tough it out" and force themselves to continue in this energy debt, the body shifts into survival or "starvation mode," a survival adaptation that taps into protein stores (muscle mass) for fuel. This is obviously unhealthy in the short and long term for an athlete. Competitive youth sports should not be mistaken for a survival test.

The nutrition key for today's active youth athletes is this: quality calories from a variety of sources throughout their day along with plenty of fluids. The demands on our athletes require that we help them make what they eat count because consistent training and performance depend on it. At the pace kids travel, today's athlete or athletic family needs to spend minimal time to get maximal nutrition.

Here are some quick ways to check on how healthy your athletes' diets are:

- Do they eat in moderation in a quantity and portion size to maintain a healthy weight?
- Do they consume a variety of foods, including 3 servings of milk or dairy, 4–5 servings of fruits or vegetables and 2 small servings of protein-rich foods daily?
- Do they eat wholesome foods, choosing natural over processed foods whenever possible?
- Do they eat at mealtimes with healthy snacks between?

- Do they eat fast food only infrequently?
- How is their energy level?
- Do they drink six 8-oz glasses of water daily rather than sugary, expensive drinks?
- Can they fight off illness or does it linger?

If you are tossing in some no's on this checklist—and, let's face it, we all can do better—here are some simple hints to encourage improved eating based on what I have observed is common among our athletes. Aim to make small changes and not to overhaul.

- Pay attention to the number and variety of servings.
- Eat from at least 3 of the 4 food groups at each meal.
- Choose by 2s each day: 2 dairy (glass of milk, serving of cheese or yogurt), 2 small proteins (PBJ, tuna, lean meat, poultry, fish), 2 large fruits and veggies (banana, apple, sweet potato)
- Find healthy combinations: cereal + milk, lean sandwich meat + cheese or egg, stir fry combo, fruit smoothies, fruit + yogurt, dried fruit + nuts
- Have healthy snacks handy at home, in the car and in their sports bag (dry cereal, trail mix, popcorn, bagels/pretzels, nuts, cookies like Fig Newtons, vanilla wafers, ginger snaps, animal crackers)

Bottom line: they're only as good as the octane in their engines. As an added bonus, not only will their sports performance improve, but we know that well-fed kids perform better in their classes and fend off illness better. It just makes sense to eat well. Life is demanding, and so are their sports. Don't let them cut corners on this one.

Game day (and tournament weekend) eating

Game day eating is both particularly important and particularly difficult. First, keep in mind that each of your athletes is an "experiment of one." They each must figure out what works best for them on game day. Provided they have a healthy everyday high carbohydrate athlete's diet with plenty of variety, here are some general guidelines for consumption prior to, during and post competition.

Be sure they start with a full "glycogen tank." The well-documented carbohydrate "loading" to fill up the glycogen stores is still advisable, though this should occur over several days before the game and not in huge quantities the night before, when it might weigh them down. Have a sports meal consisting of easily digestible food 2–4 hours before the game. This is athlete-dependent. For instance, bagels and oatmeal work for me, but yogurt doesn't.

Pre-game—to prevent lightheadedness and fatigue, settle stomachs and fuel muscles
- Choose high carb, low fat foods that digest easily (fruits, yogurt, skim milk, diluted juices or sports drinks)
- Allow adequate digestion time (at least an hour before warm-up)
- If you get the jitters and can't eat on game day, or if you have an early game, eat well the day before. And

remember that stress uses up energy. Staying calm and confident allows you to spend your energy bank wisely.

- If you have a magic food, bring it with you when you play or travel. Always eat familiar foods before competition; don't experiment.

- Drink plenty of fluids (4–8 glasses the day before, 2–3 large glasses two hours before and 1–2 glasses before kick-off, especially on hot days). If you are traveling to the game location, be sure to allow time to visit the restroom facilities.

- Avoid sugary foods that provide a quick boost of energy that plummets when you play and soft drinks that overload your absorption system. Save both for the post-game celebration.

During game/halftime—to maintain blood sugar and blood volume for muscle function and good decision-making during competition

- Drink water or sports drinks as individually tolerated. The general recommendation is 8–10 oz every 20 minutes. For competition lasting longer than an hour or for days with multiple games, sports drinks are recommended over water because they provide carbs needed to replace energy stores and electrolytes lost through perspiration. Practice drinking these during training if you plan to use them for the game. Don't risk surprises.

- Caution players to drink before they are thirsty to prevent dehydration.

Post-game—to replace fluids and minerals lost
through sweating and restore muscle fuel supplies

- Drink diluted juices to supply water and carbs. General guideline: in the first 0–2 hours target 0.5 g carbs/lb body weight; repeat 2 hours later (e.g., 130-lb player needs 65 g/260 cal by 2 hours, 130 g/520 cal by 4 hours)
- Eat watery foods like watermelon and grapes. Soups supply fluids as well as carbs, vitamins and minerals, but beware of the high sodium variety.
- Sports drinks may supply fluids and carbs but minimal vitamins and minerals.
- If there is time for a meal between games (4–6 hours), mix small portions of moderately digestible carbs with some protein and plenty of fluids. Stay away from fast food and sugary drinks. Don't confuse energy drinks with sports drinks. Energy drinks are generally very high in sugar, twice that of sports drinks, and this hampers fluid absorption.
- Rest is essential for full recovery. Minimize sun, heat and exertion.

Between games—same as halftime or pre-game,
depending on the timing of the next game's warm-up

- Stay away from fast food that is high in fat (hard to digest), salt (dehydrating), and sugar (energy spikes, then plummets).
- Replace fluids and minerals lost through sweating, and restore muscle fuel supplies.

- Even if your athletes don't feel hungry (adrenaline, heat and excitement do this), muscles need refueling. Go with fruit, granola bars and power/energy bars.
- Drinking, especially water, is essential!

Hydration

Athletes need to adopt a regular pattern of good hydration, and water is their best choice. Good hydration practices have been linked to a decreased risk of strains and may assist with cushioning in knees, vertebral discs and the brain. But in season, players should pay special attention to hydrating 12–24 hours before a match so their urine is colorless. I've seen plenty of kids try to catch up on their fluids on the long drive to the away game, only to be very disappointed that the porta-potty is their only option at the field. Word to the wise: leave extra time at away locations to make a pit stop.

On very hot days, when athletes (and their coaches) sweat a lot, dehydration is a particular risk. Humidity adds to the cooling challenge, along with midday sun and even the stress of competition. Add in lots of minutes played at high intensity and you have the recipe for sapping players' fluids. The resulting reduction in blood volume impairs cooling and "thickens" the blood, which increases the demand on hardworking hearts. On these days, "Drink before you have to" is my battle cry, and especially with female players. The boys may sweat a bit more, depending on their age, and seem to need fewer reminders to drink. Dehydration is a devious opponent. It can sneak up on athletes before they are aware of it. Even a 1% drop in fluid volume can result in a significant decline in performance. But many athletes don't experience thirst until a 2% drop in fluid levels or more, when performance capacity may be already reduced by 10–15%. Encourage—no, insist—that they drink before they're thirsty.

Be looking for the signs of dehydration: weakness, dizziness, headaches, fatigue. These may progress to cramping, chills and nausea if fluid volume drops by 5% or more. Heat illness likely accompanies these symptoms. Get them off the field and out of the sun and replenish fluids.

Safety note: dehydration is a particular concern in kids because they don't sweat as much as adults and they don't cool as efficiently. Be sure to include plenty of water breaks. Give special attention to kids carrying a few extra pounds. In everything they do, they work harder than the small kids to get it done. "Sweating off the pounds" is not the way to take off weight. It is a long-standing and dangerous exercise myth perpetuated by the people who make those plastic jogging suits. Weight lost thorough sweating will return when fluids are replaced.

I don't need to remind you that many games come down to the last seconds. The team that is fed and watered is less fatigued, maintains skills and good decision-making and is more often first to the ball. Healthy, well-nourished bodies are their foundation. Knowing they can dig deep for what's left in the tank may surprise them. But you knew the equation: quality in = quality out. Help them know it, too.

Special population: vegetarian and vegan athletes

You may have some athletes that, for health or religious reasons or because of social consciousness, choose to maintain a vegetarian diet (non-meat eating) or a vegan diet (a vegetarian diet that also excludes eggs, dairy products and all animal-derived ingredients). Indications are that a well-planned vegetarian diet can effectively support athletic performance, with some special considerations. A coach shouldn't be expected to become an amateur nutritionist or dietician, but here are some guidelines for your vegetarian/vegan athletes:

1. Vegetarians need extra protein to meet their needs for essential amino acids and iron, a crucial component of red blood cells. For women this is a particular concern. Nancy Clark recommends 60–90 mg of protein per day.[3] Vegetarians are at increased risk for non-anemic iron deficiency because plant-based iron is not as easily absorbed from the diet. Good sources are eggs, dairy, grains, nuts and soy. Here are iron-rich examples from plant-based foods:

   • Legumes: lentils, soybeans, tofu, tempeh, lima beans
   • Grains: quinoa, fortified cereals, brown rice, oatmeal
   • Nuts and seeds: pumpkin, squash, pine, pistachio, sunflower, cashews, unhulled sesame
   • Vegetables: tomato sauce, Swiss chard, collard greens
   • Other: blackstrap molasses, prune juice

   Eating these non-heme iron-containing foods along with foods rich in vitamin C (strawberries, citrus fruits, cabbage, broccoli, leafy greens, tomato sauce) can considerably

---

3   Source: http://www.ncbi.nlm.nih.gov/pubmed/15212753.

increase iron absorption. These combinations are present in, for example, beans and rice with salsa, falafel with tomatoes and hummus with lemon juice.

2. Vitamin B12 likely needs supplementing since it is found only in meat and is important for red blood cell production. Many cereals are fortified with B12.

3. Female athletes in particular tend to need more calcium from milk and dairy. Vegans can get their calcium from dark green vegetables, such as turnips and collard greens. Kale and broccoli are good plant sources when eaten in sufficient quantities. Calcium-enriched and fortified products, including juices, cereals, soy milk, soy yogurt and tofu, are other options.

Clark concludes, "What we know is that when it comes to endurance performance, it's all about the fuel, primarily carbohydrates, and you can get sufficient carbohydrates whether you're a vegetarian or a meat eater—unless you follow a really goofy diet, which some people do. It's possible to eat a lousy vegetarian diet, just as you as can eat a lousy meat-based diet. My feeling is that hard training trumps everything. Diet, if it's healthy, isn't going to make that much difference."[4]

Caution: Coaches and trainers should be aware that some athletes may adopt a vegetarian diet as a strategy for weight control. The possibility of a disordered eating pattern should be investigated if a vegetarian diet is accompanied by unwarranted weight loss.

---

4   Source: http://well.blogs.nytimes.com/2012/06/20/can-athletes-perform-well-on-a-vegan-diet/

Special population: disordered eating and eating disorders

Disordered eating is eating in a way that could or does harm you physically or psychologically. Disordered eating can be a result of a desire to lose weight, control weight, or manage emotions and can be impacted by additional familial, environmental and circumstantial factors. In athletes, the competitive environment and the drive for peak performance contribute to the risk for disordered eating behaviors. When this behavior continues over a sustained period of time, it is diagnosed as an eating disorder.

Approximately 8–10 million Americans have an eating disorder, such as anorexia or bulimia, and there are millions more who have a binge eating disorder. Eating disorders are most prevalent in adolescent and college-aged girls (only 10–15% of those affected are male), but they can affect people of any age. A person with an eating disorder is often a perfectionist, a driven and "wanting to please" person. Does this describe any of your athletes?

Every coach should know what to look for if he suspects an eating disorder among his athletes. Here are some common signs:

- Sudden, significant weight loss and/or a very strong fear of gaining five pounds
- Obvious restriction of food intake, avoiding eating with the group and/or frequent trips to the bathroom after eating
- Extreme calorie restriction
- Bingeing or vomiting
- Considering foods to be "good" or "bad"

- Visiting pro-anorexia or pro-bulimia websites
- Sad or depressed appearance or tendency to withdraw socially
- Wearing baggy clothes to hide weight loss

I encourage all coaches to visit the Renfrew Center website (http://www.renfrew.org/) to find excellent information on eating disorders and their treatment and prevention. For more information and resources for coaches, see the Resources section.

In addition to recognizing signs and symptoms, we must provide our athletes with accurate information regarding weight, weight loss, body composition, nutrition and sports performance to challenge any unhealthy practices that are counterproductive. Female athletes who engage in disordered eating put themselves at risk of menstrual irregularities, amenorrhea and female athlete triad (the confluence of disordered eating, amenorrhea and osteoporosis). Because weight is a sensitive personal issue for many women, coaches should deemphasize weighing athletes and beware of associating weight with sport performance. Explore your own values and attitudes regarding weight, dieting and body image and think about how these may inadvertently affect how you interact with your athletes. As the coach, you may be the trusted person a young person can confide in about a difficult behavioral issue. Identify a sports psychologist or eating disorder specialist in your area to whom you can refer an athlete you suspect of having an eating disorder.

According to Karin Kratina, MA, RD, from the Renfrew Center, "the annual mortality rate associated with anorexia nervosa is more than 12 times higher than the death rates of all other causes of death for females 15–24 years old." This is a serious illness with potentially severe consequences if left untreated.

Special population: celiac disease

I owe special thanks to Jeanette Corgnati and her daughter, Maggie, a longtime member of my rec league soccer teams. They introduced me to this illness nearly a decade ago and continue to inspire me with their courage and fortitude in the face of it.

Jeanette shares, "My daughter Maggie had lost 20% of her body weight in two months, and she was only two years old. She was vomiting several times a day. After many tests, we discovered Maggie had celiac disease and would need to be on a strict gluten-free diet. No medications, just eating healthy gluten-free foods, would make her well again. Amazing that food can make someone so sick."

That was 15 years ago, before there was much awareness of this illness, and Jeanette had to research it and change the way she planned and prepared meals for her family. She was also concerned about how other kids would treat her daughter and how she would manage in a "public-eating" situation.

This was how I first became aware of it: my team of six-year-olds went out for a celebration lunch at the end of the season. While all the other girls dug into their chicken nuggets and French fries, pizza and burgers, Maggie stared down at the chicken breast with broccoli on her plate; she was too small to use the restaurant silverware to cut it herself. As coach, that fell to me, the only adult in the vicinity. Maggie was quite shy, so I offered to help her, and she introduced me to an illness I never would have seen.

Celiac disease is an autoimmune disease that affects the digestive process in the small intestine. The body cannot process gluten—a protein found in wheat, rye and barley—and attacks the intestine, causing malabsorption. Symptoms include upset stomach, diarrhea, vomiting, fatigue and joint pain, and will usually occur a few hours after eating the offending grains. In extreme cases those suffering from the disease can have a very severe reaction, much like food poisoning. Continued exposure to gluten results in severe malnutrition. The good news is that the disease can be completely controlled through a gluten-free diet. Celiac disease affects at least 3 million Americans and probably many more who are yet undiagnosed.

Jeanette writes, "A person with celiac disease must avoid pretty much everything that is not fruit, vegetable or meat. They can't eat cakes, cookies, cereals or other grain products made with wheat, rye or barley and in most cases oats. [Gluten] may be hidden in candies, drinks, sauces and other items, so adhering to the diet is not always as simple as it seems. In our society of fast and pre-prepared foods, it is a bit of a challenge at first but gets easier, especially with so many gluten-free (GF) products available now. A Celiac can eat any meat, vegetable or gluten-free starch, like rice, potatoes and corn products. Meals become a focus of the day, but it also brings you back to home cooking and fresh ingredients."

Knowing that Maggie couldn't have the "normal" half-time snacks or celebration team cake, Jeanette always volunteered to be my "team Mom" in charge of these snacks. I'm not sure Maggie's teammates ever knew they were eating gluten-free cake, but I sure was glad they could all enjoy it together.

Maggie is now 17 and has been living with celiac disease for 15 years; she will never outgrow it. But she lives well with it, and it hasn't stopped her from competing successfully. She has played soccer most of her life and now competes on the high school track team, where she recently qualified for the district championships. She just brings along gluten-free snacks and her research on the local restaurants when they travel to invitational meets.

Jeanette says that, in spite of precautions, sometimes Maggie has gotten sick while traveling. But "her teammates took good care of her and rallied her. She even set a PR in her event the next day." Jeanette is convinced that "having celiac disease has made Maggie stronger and tougher than most kids." She adds, "I just wish we could control the teenage drama with a gluten-free diet!"

Jeanette shares resources on this disease and some of Maggie's favorite recipes, including team cupcakes, in Appendix E.

For more nutrition information and ways to bring nutrition education to your athletes, see the Resources section and these Appendices:

- Appendix C: Eating to Be Your Best, which includes a nutrition handout for your team, helping athletes work healthy nutrition into their busy routines
- Appendix D: Nutrition Fun FAQ Quiz, a way to engage players in the nutrition conversation
- Appendix E: Gluten-Free Recipes, a large selection of tasty and healthy gluten-free offerings

7

Beating Injuries to Keep Your Athletes in the Game

The other team isn't the only opponent our players have; injuries can be just as defeating and even more debilitating. The good coach can take steps to keep injuries to a minimum, and knows what to do when they occur. In this chapter we'll consider common soccer injuries and the coach's role in managing and reducing them.

We'll take a look at:

• Coach as first responder—should a player continue?
• Dealing with conflicting desires
• Injuries common to soccer players

- Special psychological considerations for the injured athlete
- Injury prevention as part of your game plan

Whenever I start working with a new group of kids, I always ask, "Who has something that hurts?" Immediately several hands go up. I hear a litany of "knees, ankles, back, shoulders" —complaints like they're a bunch of old folks instead of twelve-year-olds. Many have pain, and for some it's significant enough to keep them on the sidelines. What do you do with the injured kid, the kid predisposed to injury, the kid recovering from injury and the injured kid returning to play?

No kid likes to sit the bench. The game is where the fun is. We use the bench as a consequence; if someone breaks the rules, they're benched. But the kid who's hurt experiences the same consequence, except it's not his fault. Injured players are forced to sit and watch teammates do what they would love to be doing. It's more than we should ask of a kid.

Injuries to youth players used to be rare. Now they are commonplace. Any field. Any weekend. Many people involved in youth sports are raising a hue and cry and asking "why?" The list of reasons is long: poor fitness, poor training, poor nutrition, overtraining, overstressing. I've spent six chapters discussing how we can respond to this need, but we have to face the fact that injuries will happen. It doesn't get any easier as kids grow older in the game. As their strength and speed increase, their collisions are stronger and incidental contact with other players and the ground will happen. Every coach needs to be prepared in the event one of his players goes down.

Coach as first responder

As coaches we are not meant to be sports medicine experts, and we shouldn't overstep our credentials. But let's face it: we're our athletes' first responders. When they go down on the field, the referee signals us to come on and check out their condition. This is a unique privilege. Ask any parent, waved away when poised on the sidelines to charge out and carry their injured warrior off the field of battle. As parents we're inclined to rescue. As coaches we have to weigh our options.

As we run onto the field, we picture the play we just saw. What might have happened? How might the player have been hurt? Did she get clipped from behind? Did his ankle turn? Did her knee buckle? Was there a collision of heads? Of course, we are also thinking about this particular kid. Each one is his or her own case study, for sure, so we thumb through our mental file on this kid. Quick to tears? Shakes stuff off easily? The injured kid will notice how we react, so we need to monitor our own reaction to the circumstance.

When we reach them, we survey the scene. How are they lying? What are they bending or holding onto or rubbing? Or, heaven forbid, what if they are not moving? Then we have to decide what to do next.

This is my approach to triage.

1. If they are not moving and/or if you suspect any sort of neck or back injury, stop the game and call the ambulance. Bring in medical professionals immediately.
2. If there has been a collision but they can sit or stand, help them to the sidelines. If you suspect a concussion,

they are done for the day. Someone trained in concussion assessment should observe their behavior and ask questions to assess the clarity of their thinking. (For more on concussion assessment and management, see the section below and Appendix F, Care and Management of Common Injuries.)

3. If they have any reluctance about weight-bearing, assist them off the field. Enlist the help of another coach or parent if necessary.

4. On the sidelines ask them what hurts and where. I ask them to point to what hurts if they can. Have them rate the pain on a 1–10 scale. If there is extreme pain (5–10) or swelling, they can't move at a joint or you suspect a fracture or dislocation, they are done with play until they have seen a doctor and get clearance to return to play.

This is all basic stuff that even an experienced parent could accomplish. Here comes the "coaching" part. What do you do when their injury is borderline? If they have a knock or a "niggle," a localized, relatively minor discomfort?

1. Have them stand. If they are balanced and show no impairment, have them walk. If they can walk normally without favoring the injured part, ask them to jog. Watch them carefully, especially the "tough" ones, who may try to soldier through pain to get back on the field. Finally, ask them to run through moves they would have to perform on the field, reproducing game pace

and intensity as much as possible. Can they hop, cut, and jump without breaking form? If they can, they may choose to return to play.

2. If their movement is compromised, they should not return to play. Sit them down and promote them to assistant coach. Not just keeping stats but analyzing the game, the opponents' weaknesses and the places for opportunity. They have just come off the field, after all, and offer a viewpoint you can't possibly have. They may see something you've missed. This will make the bench a bit more of a tolerable place to finish the game.

Of course, injuries, while more common during competition, happen during training as well. Especially early in the season, niggles abound. Unless players are in very good physical shape they will have some initial soreness, especially in the muscles most used. The training ground is the perfect place for a coach to help kids get to know their bodies better. As they do, they will be better able to monitor what to "shake off" and what needs rest. Once they are free of pain, they can address the issue with stretching and strengthening.

The rule of thumb for aches:

1. Discomfort that diminishes with activity is generally safe to play on but should be monitored.
2. Pain that persists or enhances with activity needs rest.
3. Pain that isn't getting any better after a few days needs a professional evaluation. (See Appendix G, Communicating with a Health Care Professional.)

Dealing with conflicting desires

The news is rife with so-called "heroic" stories of athletes who have played through injury. For instance, Tiger Woods competing with a leg fracture and a torn ACL; Kerri Strugg, 1996 Olympic gymnast, landing a vault on a severely sprained ankle; and, more recently, Washington Redskins quarterback Robert Griffin III convincing his coach to let him play on a knee we saw buckle on national television. Fame, fortune, glory, honor, ego—all of these can be strong driving forces behind decisions to risk continuing play. Let's just admit that when an athlete is injured, the coach is put into a very difficult position. In deciding, he/she may have to face one the following:

- **The hyper-competitive athlete** who denies that he needs to take a seat. This is where knowing your athletes is critical and knowing yourself, even more so. If their injury and return-to-play decision is borderline, especially if this is a "big" game, default to the concrete evaluation protocol outlined above. Don't let them talk you into putting them back in if they shouldn't continue. And don't let your immediate gratification impulses, either to please them or to please your ego, talk you into making a poor decision that could cost the player more games, the whole season or more.
- **The hyper-committed/dedicated athlete** who may be responding to the weight of peer pressure. Peer pressure, real or imagined, can exert a tremendous tug on an athlete who doesn't want to appear weak or to let her teammates down. Mind over matter can get us going in the toughest

circumstances, but as coach you must assess not only whether she can continue, but whether she should. This is when you call on the trust relationship you have established with this athlete before this moment. Will she be honest with you? Have you created a safe environment for her to take a seat? Kids need to know that you won't leave them on the bench as damaged goods, that you truly value their healthy play and that you'll work to help them return full force.

- **The athlete's parent in denial** about the extent of his/her child's injury, especially if more than this game is at stake (e.g., a college scout is present, a high level coach has come to watch, the parent has his/her own ego invested in the kid's performance). Adults will actually put their kids in harm's way when they bring an unbalanced perspective to the field, even though they believe they are "doing their best" for the kid. Start there, by recognizing their intentions, but hold firm to your decision-tree protocol and your gut instinct about the kid and the family. This always works better if you have introduced your "triage protocol" ahead of time at a team meeting when level heads ruled the day. If a college coach is truly interested in a player, he or she will make time to come watch on another day when the athlete is playing full force. If this is the kind of coach who expects kids to play through injury, your athlete doesn't want to play for that coach.
- **The oblivious or inexperienced parent** who doesn't see what you see. If you've taken a player out, or even if you haven't but you have some concerns about how his or

her body is performing, be sure and communicate these concerns to the parent. Don't presume they know, and don't assume players will tell their parents what you have told them. Coach-to-parent communication is often quite limited, especially as players reach middle school and high school age. Information about player health should be a face-to-face conversation if at all possible to head off misunderstandings that happen through emails and phone messages. Tell the parent, "you may want to watch this ankle, knee, leg," "be alert for signs of concussion" or "have him evaluated if injury symptoms linger." (See Appendix F, Care and Management of Common Injuries.)

- **Your own internal conflict.** Let's be honest. If this is an impact player and it's a critical time in an important game, you will be tempted to let her continue playing even if she shouldn't. Don't let your desire to win today's game sway your decision about this kid's potential future. Doing the right thing, especially when it's the hard thing, is always inspiring. Good teams dig deep when they do it for their injured teammate.

Strugg, Woods and RGIII, while laudable (and highly paid), really should not be our role models and certainly not our standards. The kids who have been entrusted to our care and tutelage need us to take the long view. A compromised movement pattern means weakness and perhaps subconscious "favoring" by the rest of the body. This significantly increases the risk of injury. Young athletes, though they may beg to get back in there, are not able to see things this way. After all, without a mirror they can't see themselves move. You have to be this mirror for them.

Injuries common to soccer players

The list of potential injuries for our youth soccer players is unfortunately quite long. Some are minor, like generalized soreness, muscle cramps, and side stitches, and are relatively easy to manage. Some, like scrapes, bruises, cuts and contusions, may require a bit of first aid. (See Appendix H for first aid and how to stock your med kit.) Some, when there is significant pain or swelling and/or you suspect a fracture or dislocation, obviously require the care and advice of a medical professional. The American Red Cross offers Sports Training Safety courses for coaches (http://www.redcross.org/take-a-class).

The injuries most difficult for the coach to address are the ones where the player may be able to "play through" them but you're not sure whether they should. The majority of these are musculoskeletal in nature and fall into one of these categories: sprains, strains, tears. (See Glossary for definitions.) For these injuries it is critical for the coach to recognize the extent of a potentially harmful injury and advise the athlete and his family on the best course of action to ensure the health of the child.

Here is a listing of the most common injuries grouped by body part:

- Head/neck: concussion
- Hip/thigh: groin pulls, hamstring strains, IT band inflammation, quad pulls

- Knee: anterior cruciate ligament (ACL), medial collateral ligament (MCL), posterior collateral ligament (PCL) strain or tear, meniscus injury, patellofemoral pain syndrome
- Leg/shin: shin splints, stress fracture, compartment syndrome
- Ankle/foot: ankle sprain, plantar fasciitis, Achilles tendonitis, Sever's disease
- Misc: muscle cramps, heat injury

See Appendix F, Care and Management of Common Injuries, for what the coach needs to know about:

- The anatomy of the injury
- Its symptoms and causes, with special consideration for the young athlete
- Its care and management
- Training and play that might increase the likelihood of the injury
- Recommendations for training design to help protect your players from the injury

While we'd like to prevent all injuries, let's focus on two that are currently plaguing the youth ranks: concussions and ACL tears. These two injuries are not only taking kids out of play but also impacting their lives and potentially their futures. I'll discuss both injuries below and offer a detailed training design for reducing these injuries in the appendix.

Concussion

As many as 3.8 million recreational and sports-related concussions are reported annually in this country, and that number has skyrocketed in the last decade. Sport science is rushing to study the sudden rise in incidence and severity of this injury. Right behind football players, soccer players swell the ranks of the injured, with girls' risk double that of boys' in comparable sports. Soccer and basketball rank 1 and 2, respectively, for girls.

Concussion is a mild traumatic brain injury that occurs as the result of a blow to the head or to the body with force transmitted to the head. It's an acceleration of the brain inside the skull (whiplash-like) that results in temporarily impaired brain function. Let me not downplay the significance of this injury: it is a shaking of the brain that may disrupt brain cell nerve transmission in visual, spatial and executive function regions. It may even cause a shearing of the nerves that run between the brain's two hemispheres. It's serious. We now realize that young, growing brains are particularly susceptible to this type of injury.

We used to call this "getting your bell rung." Players wore as a badge of honor their ability to tough this out and keep going. It's still happening. I recently heard a girl compliment an opponent, "Hey, way to take a hit." Valor and toughness are admired and encouraged in athletics. This discourages players from reporting their symptoms; they don't want to come out of the game. That means coaches and parents who understand the risk of cumulative, long-term and even permanent effects have to turn up their vigilance and pay special attention to players after a collision or hard hit. The players themselves may not be aware anything is wrong, but their immediate behavior after impact often gives them away: a shake of the head, rubbing the temple, blinking the eyes to clear vision.

Part of the challenge we face is that we have been conditioned to think of youth as maximally resilient. They bounce back better than adults from most injuries, but they are particularly susceptible to this one. This injury is unique because it is "invisible." Even medical imaging studies can't "see" the damage done to brain tissue or brain circuitry; injury can't be measured, only presumed from the athlete's reports, behavior and sensation. The athlete himself may not know he is concussed. That means the coach is an exceedingly important first responder.

Coaches should:

- Educate themselves about concussive symptoms.
- Teach proper heading technique, including good body position in the air.
- Include neck, upper back and shoulder strengthening, especially for female players (http://fit2finish.com/strengthening-our-girls-against-concussions-three-simple-ways-to-build-neck-and-core-strength-while-keeping-it-fun/).
- Encourage all players to report any symptoms to you. Teammates don't let teammates play with a concussion. Do not let them return to play until they are cleared, even if player or parent insists.
- Educate players and parents about this injury. Helpful information, links and handouts can be found here: http://www.cdc.gov/concussion/HeadsUp/youth.html

Parents should:

- Monitor their child for symptoms, even if they haven't heard about any collisions.
- Have kids checked out by a medical professional experienced in treating concussions if they complain of any symptoms or show persistent (beyond teen-normal) irritability or are especially emotional, nervous, sad, confused or fatigued.
- Be aware that girls may be more likely to complain of drowsiness and sensitivity to noise, boys of amnesia and confusion.
- Take advantage of baseline pre-season concussion screening offered through schools and community health professional organizations. These reports are valuable should the child experience a concussive event.

Athletes should:

- Report to coach, parent or athletic trainer any symptoms that arise after a collision, fall or impact to the body.
- Notice if a teammate, who may not realize it, exhibits symptoms of a concussion.
- If you have a concussion, rest your brain the way you would rest an injured muscle—completely, until it's ready to return to action.

Some medical professionals are recommending that heading be abandoned in soccer, but most soccer coaching and training professionals believe this is an unnecessary precaution that would completely change the game. A few doctors recommend eliminating heading before a certain age, but this would prevent kids from learning proper heading technique in a safe, lower contact environment. A number of companies make large claims for the safety offered by head gear, but so far none has been shown to protect against concussion. Collisions occur regardless of heading and so does forceful incidental contact.

Today's sport science recommends teaching kids how to head the ball correctly, preparing them with strength and coordination to do this safely and effectively and insisting they play the game with respect for their own physical health and that of their opponents. The reason why today's young brains seem so fragile in this regard is currently an area of intense study.

ACL injuries

Injuries to the knee, particularly non-contact injuries to the anterior cruciate ligament (ACL), continue to occur at alarming rates among young soccer players. The risk is 4–6 times greater in women than in men. Of NCAA women soccer players, more than one athlete in ten suffers a serious knee injury. Of high school athletes, the injury rate is more than one in a hundred, representing more than 20,000 injuries each year.

Comprehensive plyometric training and dynamic warm-up programs like those presented in Chapters 4 and 5 can considerably reduce this risk. Ongoing studies show that these programs, performed correctly, can significantly reduce the risk of ACL injury to women soccer players' knees, but these injuries still plague our youth athletes. In fact, they are now occurring in younger and younger kids. In addition, studies of young adults performed 10 to 20 years after ACL repair show that they are experiencing significant osteoarthritis in their previously repaired knees.

This is one injury we can't just keep treating. We've got to prevent it. As a coach, you can lead this charge with your players.

Commit to:

- 15 minutes of ACL prevention warm-ups before every practice and every game.
- Include injury prevention "movement" as part of practice and play.
- If you coach elementary-aged kids, focus on balance, body control and agility, which are "pre-injury prevention" movement skills.
- With middle school kids and older, instruct and expect the "three B's" (Bend your knees, Balls of your feet, Be Balanced, heads up and ready to play) in all practice drills.
- Insist on perfect form for the exercises, and enroll your players in the commitment.
- Observe your players to be sure they transfer these movement patterns to their game play. Design drills to imitate game situations, just as you would technical and tactical training.

In their training and play look for:

- Bending at the knees and not from the waist
- Keeping knees from bowing inwards on cutting and landing
- Agility, quickness and playing "light on their feet"
- Athleticism, smooth movement, body control and disciplined play

Insert basic strengthening to:

- Build a strong core and good endurance
- Maintain supple, responsive muscles and full range of motion at joints

Fifteen minutes of a well-designed, well-executed training program really is worth your time. You can run these programs and kids enjoy performing them. This will give kids a fighting chance to keep playing the game they love, in the spirit and with the intensity it deserves.

Special considerations for the injured athlete

Unfortunately, not all injuries are preventable. When they do occur, they present some special challenges for the athlete and coach, both during the injury layoff and when managing the athlete's return to play. The coach should be aware of the following:

- **The psychological toll an injury takes** on an athlete who loves to play and now can't. Both their team identity and their personal identity may be wrapped up in that uniform. Sitting on the bench in street clothes is a lonely feeling. Invite them to participate as statistician or strategist on the sidelines to help them continue to feel part of the team.

- **The potential pressure an athlete may feel, whether self-imposed or from a parent or respected coach, to return to play sooner than they should.** Physicians are now recognizing that a host of repeat ACL injuries may be due to early return to play. Know the recommended protocol to bring the player gradually back up to speed. Consult with the athlete's sports medicine professional about when he/she will be released to participate. Be clear about plans for the player to rejoin the team and at what level of exertion, as well as the time course for reintroduction to full contact.

- **The significant effects of de-training** during the layoff. Often athletes get the nod from their physician to return to doing "whatever they want" or "general activities," not recognizing that the athlete translates this to mean jumping back into action. "General activities" means they can take the bus and walk to class. It does not mean they can play full minutes in the next game or even go full steam in the next practice. Their cardiovascular fitness will be diminished depending on how long they were out, and their proprioception (body sense), neuromuscular coordination and timing will be off. In activities like soccer that demand quickness and agility, a split-second delay will set them off balance. Insist that they start slowly at a point where they are balanced and capable, and start building back from there. The same goes for cardio; they may be surprised at how much they need to recover. This will require their time and patience and yours. Don't rush things.

- **The likelihood of fear or reluctance upon first returning from injury.** Athletes may not trust their body to do what it used to do. This is a healthy fear and will dissipate as they become reacquainted with their old, capable selves. They may need extra time with basic moves and drills. Hold off on full pressure and tackles until the athlete indicates that he is ready.

Can we keep them from getting injured?

We'd all agree that healthy is better than hurt, and that the playing field is better than the sidelines. In the ER, a pound of cure is WAY more expensive than a pound of prevention. Unfortunately, taking time for injury prevention can be a very hard sell. When I first launched my fitness and injury prevention business, I went straight to experienced coaches, especially those who coached young women, and said, "I have training that will help protect your players." These coaches politely informed me that "injuries are just a part of the game" and thanked me for my concern. They knew the game, the skills, the drills, and the motivational pep talks, but they didn't know health and fitness.

Most coaches aren't aware that many, if not most, of the injuries sustained by our youth athletes are preventable. Unfortunately, coaches who are not trained in the principles of fitness and movement (chapters 2 and 3) don't realize that simply by being smart and forward-looking about the way we train our athletes, we could nearly eliminate the risk of many of the injuries we used to consider just an "inevitable part of the game." You are not "most coaches." Now you have the tools to put injury prevention into play.

For more information see these appendices:

- Appendix F: Care and Management of Common Injuries, a "cheat sheet" of 14 common soccer injuries, their symptoms and management, and best strategies for prevention
- Appendix G: Communicating with a Health-Care Professional
- Appendix H: First Aid and How to Pack Your Med Kit

Conclusion:
Fit to the Finish

Can the demanding environment of youth sports today still be a healthy place for kids to play? Absolutely. When kids are guided by a capable parent or coach who helps them find a good fit for their skills and their desire, youth sports can be both healthy and fun. Sure, we'd like to have winners. But first let's get this generation of young athletes hooked on playing the game. Before they know it, they'll be fitter, healthier, more athletic and more confident. Sounds like winning to me.

This handbook has offered 7 chapters with one objective: to help your players be fit to the finish, particularly for soccer. As we've seen, kids present a special opportunity. They are young and impressionable, open to ideas and ready for most anything. But with opportunity comes challenge; they're growing, and they need special care and handling.

Attrition, injury and selection processes are driving our kids out of the game. Let's face it: they have plenty of other choices that are less demanding and much more convenient. Our job as coaches and teachers of the game is to make it worth choosing. How? By welcoming what they bring and helping them discover what the game has to offer.

As coach, mentor and role model, we have a unique opportunity to walk kids through this. Teach them to play to their strengths, work on their weaknesses, and be patient, yet persistent. Help them evaluate their game to see their progress and celebrate the improvements they've made. All this will help prepare them for whatever comes next: the tough opponent, the team tryout, the school bully, the parents' divorce.

Of course, we keep reevaluating, just like we keep reworking the lineup and adjusting the game plan, some days on the fly. We want them to find their place in the game, a healthy fit and not a forced fit. We want them to grow and improve and discover their potential.

This is where the individual coach-athlete relationship you've built is indispensable. To be a good guide and mentor, you need to be open to what each kid needs from the game. What are they playing for? Different kids, different goals. You may have 'em all on the same team, but where do they best fit?

- Recreational level: fun and friends, a physical break in their day (fitness for health)

- Competitive level: challenge, skills, fun and friends, competition (fitness with a purpose)
- Elite level: challenge, achievement, scholarship, fun and friends (fitness as a goal)
- College/professional level: achievement, pride, identity (fitness as a lifestyle)

Each level attracts a different kind of player and comes with its own demands; fitness to meet those demands must be part of the package. Add endurance, strength, speed, balance and flexibility to the dribbling, passing, shooting and defending you're already doing. Be sure to sprinkle in a healthy expectation for attitude, coachability and sportsmanship. The healthy game demands it all and fields it, literally, in pursuit of the goal. It's worth the investment of time because the kids are worth it. This foundation will make your coaching and their play more effective. Oh yeah, and more fun, since success is always more fun, whether it's kicking the ball more, scoring more goals or winning more tournaments.

A wise investor puts his money in the long-term growth stock. That's what fun and fitness will be for these kids. What a great investment for their long-term gains! Oh, it won't all be gain. Even the fittest teams fall short sometimes. Ups and downs are part of the sports experience. That's what makes it a great place to grow capable kids who navigate well. They'll learn a lot about themselves in the process.

That's why I'm convinced that not only is youth sports a healthy place, it's a place we can't afford to lose. There are plenty of kids out there who learn best by doing and are most teachable when they're active. I was one of those kids; perhaps you were, too. The lessons I learned there I learned for keeps. But we have to keep them playing, and playing healthy, all the way to the final whistle.

The coach's basic game plan is simple:

1. Design your training to incorporate both skills and fitness.
2. Prepare your athletes to achieve but avoid rushing performance, which risks over-training and burnout.
3. Employ injury prevention drills and implement policies for safe return to play.

Over my lifetime of playing, spectating, coaching and training athletes, I have watched youth sports evolve from a playground to a training ground, and nearly into a war zone. Often our motivated, healthy young people hit the field not quite ready for what they find there. Well-intentioned coaches get swept up in the competitive whirlwind and lose a bit of focus. Some lose their way.

The "win at all costs" environment that today's youth coaches face may deceive us into short-term thinking. For the health of our kids and our own health and perspective as coaches, we must keep the long view.

John Wooden, renowned coach of the UCLA men's college basketball team from 1948–1975, was asked on the occasion of his retirement, "Coach, who was your best player of all time?" He famously replied, "Ask me in 20 years."

Coach Wooden had a very long view. He called himself a teacher of the game, even when everyone else affectionately called him "coach." Neither profession is highly paid, but the rewards are fantastic. They'll outlast us all. John Wooden's legacy speaks for itself, and so do his former players.

Some say youth sports are a lost cause; I'm not buying it. There are millions of kids, all sizes and shapes, who need us to take back the field and offer a place for every kid to play.

We can do this by keeping our focus here:

Focus #1: We must *develop* our athletes by encouraging and motivating them to grow at their own pace in the game. This is often not a continuous climb but rather a staggered ledge-to-ledge phenomenon. They attack the rock face while we belay the rope. Let's be patient with kids, even if it means putting the win in jeopardy.

Focus #2: We must *balance* our athletes. Imbalanced stresses invite injury: right vs. left, front vs. back, start vs. stop, give vs. take, stretch vs. strengthen, push vs. pull. All of these can be taught, conditioned and put into play. Let's design our training with the whole athlete in mind, and not just for this team, this season or this sport.

Focus #3: We must *observe* our athletes. Their skills, reactions and responses are cues to their readiness for more challenge or less. Both options need to be okay. A keen eye will also identify weaknesses and imbalances before they become injuries. Let's insist on safe, skilled play and always expect the very best from our athletes.

It all boils down to the cycle of success for all of our athletes: Develop—balance—observe—repeat.

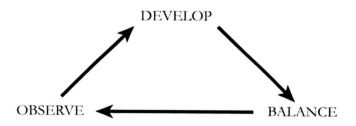

Figure 7. The cycle of success

A coach who observes, sows balance and is committed to the development of his players is patient to teach, start slowly and gradually to build on yesterday's success. He sees injury before it happens and heads it off before it gets there. This is the best long-range winning strategy.

The creative magic of successful coaching is simple. Offer them strong, healthy, sustained progress, but keep the fun. Be the coach who:

- Challenges players to do all they can,
- Pulls them back in time to regroup and recover, and then
- Re-launches them with new confidence and competitive fire.

Before you know it, they'll be asking it of themselves. Then, just get out of the way and enjoy the game. That's good coaching.

Make Fit2Finish part of your coaching game plan and help your athletes to be fit for the race, all the way to the finish line.

I'd love to hear from you as you put these principles into practice. Visit our website at http://www.fit2finish.com, contact us by e-mail at Fit2Finish05@gmail.com, or find us on:

- Facebook: https://www.facebook.com/Fit2Finish
- Twitter: https://twitter.com/Fit2Finish
- LinkedIn: http://www.linkedin.com/pub/wendy-lebolt/16/b34/47a

Yours in healthy sports,
Wendy

Acknowledgments

I guess it was my mom who first introduced me to sports, and she was my biggest supporter. She took me to games and tournaments, to practices and tryouts, and picked me up when I was done. It never occurred to me that any field of play was off-limits or any team out of reach for a kid with good hands, decent footwork, some field sense and a desire to work hard. Mom has left us, but no one would be more pleased than she to know that I am still playing and paying forward what she brought to life.

But writing a book about what I do would never have happened were it not for Laurie (Dels) Phillips, who generously offered her daughter as my demo for a coaching talk and greeted me afterward with a hug and a "You gotta write that book." Then she received each chapter with enthusiasm, encouraging the next one into being. She's been in my corner all the way.

Writing a book to and for coaches was inspired by Coach Gerardo Ramirez and his team in Vienna, VA. His love of the game and his affection for his players spurred his desire to learn more about the fitness and injury prevention he wanted for his team. I feel very fortunate that he invited me to work alongside him. I have learned so much from him and the girls of the VYS Strikers Red, some of whom are featured in the video links in chapter 4.

Many, many thanks, too, go to all the dedicated coaches who have invited Fit2Finish to their practice fields over the years. Special and longtime support has come from Lisa Bishop, Rich Gleason, Mike Jorden, Kimo Kaloi, Tim Gorgos, Dennis Sixbey, John Cuellar and Svain Ulvedal.

A very special thank you to Diane Drake, head coach of the George Mason University Women's Soccer team, dedicated sport parent and dear friend. Her insight into the ranks of high level coaching, coupled with her command of the game and her clear view of the club soccer environment, was invaluable in shaping my approach to this book, assuring me that it was a book that needed writing.

Big thanks, also, to my friends in time of need. Linda DeLia, for early editing support. Vicky Hipsely, who came out of retirement to be my medical illustrator. Becky Kendall, who kindly edited tons of footage to punch up the video. And the VYS Strikers and VYS Fire for their time in shooting the video. I am also indebted to orthopedist Steve Pournaras, MD, and physical therapist Sean Mccumiskey, who offered additions and corrections for Appendix F: Care and Management of Common Injuries.

To the team at Morgan James Publishing: thanks for taking a chance on a new author with an entrepreneurial track record. Special thanks to editor extraordinaire Amanda Rooker and her cohort Ben Rooker at SplitSeed, who brought me to the finish line.

And finally to my husband Scot and daughters Jodi, Stephanie and Olivia, who have tolerated my antics on the field and celebrated my small successes along the way: you are the ones who have made me Fit 2 Finish. You will always be my perfect team.

About the Author

Wendy LeBolt, PhD, brings 23 years of soccer parenting, 15 years of soccer coaching, advanced degrees in education and exercise physiology, and 10 years of college teaching in exercise and sport science. All of this is layered over a lifetime of sports and fitness which is the language she speaks through Fit2Finish, the company she founded in 2001. For nearly a decade and a half she has trained thousands of young athletes and teams in the Washington, DC metro area and mid-Atlantic region.

Dr. LeBolt has published hundreds of articles and columns for online newsletters, magazines and news media on topics related to health, wellness, fitness and sports performance. She writes weekly for Soccerwire.com; provides a wide variety of articles, videos, and sport science information for youth sports at her website, Fit2Finish (http://www.Fit2Finish.com); and posts regularly to her inspirational blog, The Kinesthetic Christian, found here: http://kinestheticchristian.wordpress.com.

Appendix A:
Target Heart Rate Calculation

Calculating Target Heart Rate using the Karvonen Method

Target Heart Rate = [(maximal HR – resting HR) × %Intensity] + resting HR

- To estimate maximal heart rate, use 220 – age (e.g., for a 20-year-old, max HR = 220 – 20 = 200).
- If resting heart rate (HR) is unknown, use 70 bpm.
- For best measure of individualized resting HR, count the number of beats for 60 seconds upon first waking. Do this on several days to get an average resting HR.

Appendix B:
Overtraining Signs, Symptoms and Prevention

What are the signs and symptoms of overtraining?

1. Increase in resting heart rate (taken before getting out of bed in the morning for at least 10 consecutive days).
2. Persistent muscle soreness.
3. Fatigue. Reluctance to train. Body is tired and heavy. Pattern of skipping practices or games.
4. Sleeplessness. Trouble falling asleep, waking during the night.
5. Decrease in appetite. Weight loss. Irregular menstruation in females.
6. More frequent colds, upper respiratory infections.
7. Boredom. Lack of motivation. May have falling grades.
8. Decrease in self-esteem. Unhappiness that pervades other activities.
9. Cynicism. Negative outlook. Moodiness. Inappropriate response to usual stresses.
10. Frequent minor injuries. Injuries that are slow to heal or that recur.

What can I do to prevent overtraining injuries?

1. Tune into your body. Don't ignore pain—especially sharp pain or joint pain.
2. Start training at least 6-8 weeks before your season starts. Be sure to allow 10–14 days for heat acclimatization.
3. Do not increase training more than 10% per week.
4. Get 8 hours of sleep.
5. Don't skip meals. Include 1500 mg/day of calcium. Drink recommended volume of fluids.
6. Include regular stretching before and after training.
7. Take an "off-season" (maybe just making your primary sport secondary for a season).
8. Have injuries evaluated and treated. Have a sports medicine professional identify strength and/or flexibility imbalances and weaknesses. These are your "weakest links." Focus your pre-season training here.

Appendix C:

Eating to Be Your Best

Nutrition Worksheet

Begin by answering the following questions:

1. What is your favorite pre-training, pre-game food?
2. What does diet mean? (Hint: diet affects performance and consistent training.)
3. What's a calorie? (Answer: a unit of energy.)

Signs your diet may not be meeting your needs include: low energy, lingering or frequent illness, and poor performance despite substantial training effort.

Calculating your daily caloric needs

1. Body weight in lbs. x 10
2. Add 100 calories/mile (~10 cal/minute exercise)
3. Add 70% to #1 if you're very active (other than training)
   Add 50% to #1 if you're moderately active
   Add 30% to #1 if you mostly sit and chill

We need good eating practices for training diets as well as specific preparation for game days. Today, how many of you had:

3 servings of milk?

4 fruits/veggies?

Keys to healthful eating

1. Variety: vary the type of food you eat if you tend to be habitual. Go for different colors, textures, sources.

2. Moderation: nothing is absolutely excluded. Just look to balance your food intake with mostly healthy choices.

3. Wholesomeness: choose natural over processed foods when possible.

Good nutrition game plan (for everyday)

- Dairy (3-4 servings: 8 oz low fat milk, yogurt, 1.5 oz low fat cheese)
    - o Why? Bones are growing in length and density. Sufficient calcium can protect against muscular cramps.
- Fruits and vegetables (2 large or 4 smaller servings/day: oranges, bananas, melons, broccoli, spinach, green peppers, tomatoes)
    - o Why? Promotes healing and aids in exercise recovery.
- Meats and protein-rich alternatives (2 small servings/day, such as 4-6 oz lean meat, fish or poultry; or 2 servings nuts or beans)
    - o Why? Muscles are developing; also improves healing and decreases the risk of iron-deficient anemia.

- Grains and starches (4 servings/day: cereal, wholesome bread, pasta, rice)
  - Why? Fuels muscles and protects against fatigue.

Some quick check suggestions

- Eat from at least 3 of 4 food groups at each meal.
- Choose by 2s each day: 2 dairy, 2 glasses of milk, 2 small protein (PB, tuna, sandwich meat), 2 large fruits/veggies (OJ, dinner salad), 2/3 of your dinner plate is carbs

Recommended proportions of nutrients

- Carbohydrates: 65% dietary calories
- Proteins: 10-15% dietary calories
  - To calculate RDA: weight in lbs x 0.6g/lb = daily g protein

Efficient eating—ways to get both in combination

- Cereal + milk
- Sandwich with meat, cheese, egg
- Meat, poultry, shrimp stir fry
- Fruit smoothies
- Fruit and yogurt
- Dried fruit and nuts

Quick take-home cheat sheet (especially for female athletes)

- Consume enough calcium from low fat sources
- Consume enough iron; food sources rather than supplements are best

- Eat enough calories, not too many. Beware of very low calorie diets that may result in menstrual irregularities, compromised performance and brittle bones.
- Eat a variety of foods. Variability in color is a good indicator.
- Hydrate with water. Recover with sport drinks.
- Don't punish yourself for the occasional treat. Just choose your food well most of the time.

Appendix D:

Nutrition Fun FAQ Quiz

1. Vegetarians cannot get complete protein needs.
True or false?
Answer: false. Vegetarians/non-meat eaters can get complete proteins with food combinations:

- Grains + milk (cereal and milk, pasta and cheese, bread and cheese)
- Grains + beans and legumes (rice and beans, croutons and split pea soup, tortillas and beans, cornbread and chili beans, brown bread and baked beans)
- Legumes + seeds (hummus made from mashed chickpeas and sesame seeds, tofu and sesame seeds)

Note: They need to be sure they get sufficient calcium, zinc and Vitamin B_2/riboflavin, which assist with the breakdown of carbs and fats for energy.

2. What is the most important meal of the day and should be about 1/3 of your daily calories?

Answer: breakfast. No time? Pack it the night before—crackers, nuts, fruits, smoothie.

Not hungry in the a.m.? Eating late the night before? Take a mid-morning snack.

3. Snacks are unhealthy and lead to weight gain. True or false?

Answer: false.

Healthy snacks:	Low-fat cookie choices:
Dry cereal	Vanilla wafers
Raisins, dried fruits	Animal crackers
Popcorn	Ginger snaps
Muffins—homemade is best	Fig Newtons
Bagels/pretzels	
Nuts, seeds	

4. I can be healthiest with an all-carb diet because Atkins was wrong! True or false?

Answer: false. While a diet composed of lots of carbs, especially wholesome, non-processed carbs, can be low calorie, it may not be healthy. Beware of fat-free foods, which may be high in "empty" calories. The body needs a portion of proteins and some fats. It is also important to eat a variety of foods to get the necessary vitamins and minerals. Athletes with celiac disease cannot eat foods containing gluten. Some recipes that will meet their dietary needs are included in the section below. Note: if you have a gluten-free kid on your team, have that kid make the team cake for parties. Then everyone can have a piece!

5. If you're injured and unable to exercise for a week or two, your muscle will turn to fat. True or false?

Answer: false. Muscle and fat are two different tissue types; they cannot convert from one to the other. Calories consumed above and beyond the energy demands of the body will be stored as subcutaneous fat and in adipose tissue, available for future energy needs. Muscle tissue that is not used loses tone and, after some time, will atrophy and appear to shrink. It will recover its shape and volume upon return to activity.

6. Not such a fun fact: Studies show that _?_ of college female athletes suffer from disordered eating.

Answer: one third. Disordered eating can include anorexia, bulimia, laxative abuse, excess-ercise, crash diets, unhealthy weight-loss practices, and more.

I have heard of college track and cross country runners competing for who can eat the least. The "winner" had only one carrot stick. Feed your body and it will thank you. If you suspect you are headed toward disordered eating or a coach or teammate makes this suggestion, get help from a health professional.

Appendix E:
Gluten-Free Recipes

White Chocolate Chip Brownies

2 eggs	⅓ cup chocolate chips
¾ cup sugar	½ tsp. xanthan gum
¼ cup butter	¼ cup soy flour
2 oz. white chocolate	½ cup potato starch
1 tsp. baking powder	½ tsp. vanilla*

Melt butter and chocolate over low heat or in a double boiler. Beat eggs and sugar until fluffy and pale. Add vanilla and then melted butter/white chocolate. Beat well. Add dry ingredients and beat until smooth. Bake in a greased 8 x 8 pan at 325 degrees for 25–30 minutes.

Makes 16 brownies.

*Gluten Free Vanilla Extract

1 vanilla bean (split)
½ cup potato vodka

Place in covered jar—set aside for 3 weeks. Beans may be reused once or twice.

Pizzelles and Waffles

Pizzelles:

¼ cup butter, melted	1 egg
⅓ tsp. baking powder	¼ cup sugar
¼ tsp. vanilla	⅛ tsp. xanthan gum

⅓ cup gluten-free flour mix (2 parts rice flour, ⅓ part tapioca, ⅔ part potato starch)

Beat eggs and sugar until fluffy. Add vanilla and melted butter then dry ingredients. Beat well. Drop rounded spoonfuls onto preheated and greased (brushed with corn oil) pizzelle maker. Bake 1 minute or so until golden. Leave flat or shape like bowls or ice cream cones by placing warm pizzelle in a bowl or rolling it in the shape of a cone, then cool. Delicious with drizzled chocolate, whipped cream and fruit as well as ice cream.

Makes about a dozen large pizzelles.

Waffles: add 1 more egg and ¼ cup milk to mixture and cook on greased waffle iron until golden.

Sugar Cookies

½ cup cornstarch	1 tsp. vanilla
½ cup white rice flour	½ cup butter, softened
½ cup potato starch	2 egg whites
¼ cup corn flour	¼ tsp. baking powder
¼ cup tapioca starch	¾ cup sugar
½ tsp. xanthan gum	

Cream butter and sugar. Add egg whites and then dry ingredients. Wrap dough in plastic wrap and refrigerate at least 2 hours. Roll out dough between 2 pieces of wax paper coated lightly with potato starch to a thickness of about ⅛–¼ inch (not too thin or too delicate; not too thick or too doughy). Place cutouts on sheets lined with parchment paper and bake at 375 degrees for 8–10 minutes. They will not turn golden; they will remain white in color. Cool and decorate with royal icing and sprinkles. *Really good*, a family favorite!

Magical Peanut Butter Cookies

1 cup creamy peanut butter
1 egg
1 cup sugar
1 tsp. vanilla
30–36 Hershey Kisses

Cream together. Roll into 1 inch balls and roll in sugar. Bake on greased cookie sheet for 8 minutes at 350 degrees. Remove cookies and place unwrapped Hershey Kiss in center. Place back in oven for another 2–3 minutes.

Jellyrolls

4 eggs, separated
¼ cup potato starch
¼ cup tapioca starch

1 tsp. baking powder
⅔ cup sugar

For chocolate cake: cut starches in half (⅛ cup of each) and add ¼ cup cocoa.

Preheat oven to 375 degrees. Grease a 10 x 15 x 1 pan and then line with parchment paper. Grease paper as well. Beat egg yolks and sugar until thick and pale in color. Add sifted dry ingredients, stirring lightly to combine. Beat egg whites and a pinch of sugar until thick and then fold into the batter. Pour into prepared pan and bake 15–20 minutes until slightly golden and springy to the touch. Turn out onto a dish towel coated with powdered sugar. Roll cake in coated towel and let cool. When cool, unroll cake and fill with jam, whipped cream, ice cream, etc., and re-roll. Decorate the top with icing or whipped cream.

Team Party Yellow Cake

¼ cup Crisco	¼ cup potato starch &
¾ cup sugar	¼ cup corn starch
2 eggs	¼ cup tapioca starch
¾ tsp. vanilla	1 ¾ tsp. baking powder
¼ tsp. salt	½ tsp. xanthan gum
½ cup milk	

Cream Crisco and sugar until fluffy. Add eggs and vanilla and mix well. Add milk and then dry ingredients. Beat until fluffy and thick. Pour into lined muffin tins, or into prepared pan greased and lightly coated with potato starch. Bake at 350 degrees for 25–30 minutes until golden and toothpick comes out clean. Decorate with buttercream and enjoy!

Makes 10–12 medium cupcakes or double recipe for regular box cake size!

Buttercream Icing

4 tbs. meringue powder	⅔ cups warm water
1 tsp. vanilla	2 cups powdered sugar

Beat meringue powder and water to stiff peaks. Add sugar. Next add:

1 cup Crisco	½ lb butter (2 sticks, softened)
2 ½–3 cups powdered sugar	

Beat until fluffy and light. Color as desired and pipe on cake. (½ recipe will be fine for cupcakes; full for a cake)

Crumb Cake

1 box gluten-free yellow cake mix

Follow recipe and put crumb topping on with 10 minutes left.

Topping:

¼ cup sugar

¾ cups gluten-free flour

1 tsp. cinnamon

5 tbs. butter, soft

Mix together all topping ingredients and place on cake with 10 minutes left.

Chocolate Cream Cheese Brownies

2 eggs   ¼ cup cocoa powder

¾ cup sugar   ½ tsp. xanthan gum

¼ cup butter   ¼ cup soy flour

2 oz. dark chocolate   ¼ cup potato starch

1 tsp. baking powder   ½ tsp. vanilla

Cream Cheese Swirl: Cream together 3 oz cream cheese, 1 egg, ¼ cup sugar, ½ tbs. cornstarch, ½ tsp vanilla and 2 tbs. butter, and swirl with knife.

Melt butter and chocolate over low heat or in a double boiler. Beat eggs and sugar until fluffy and pale. Add vanilla and then melted butter/dark chocolate. Beat well. Add dry ingredients and beat until smooth. Pour in a greased 8 x 8 pan. Swirl in cream cheese mixture. Bake at 325 degrees for 25–30 minutes.

Makes 16 brownies.

Chocolate Chip Muffins

¼ cup butter, melted   ½ cup sugar

1 egg   1 cup gluten-free flour

½ tsp. baking powder   ½ tsp. baking soda

½ cup sour cream   ½ tsp. vanilla

¼ tsp. xanthan gum   ⅓ cup chocolate chips

Beat butter, sugar and eggs until fluffy. Add vanilla and sour cream and then dry ingredients and chips. Pour into greased muffin tins and bake at 350 degrees for 15–20 minutes until golden.

(Makes 8 small muffins; double for 12 larger ones)

Pizza Dough

½ cups rice flour

1 egg

1 tbs. yeast

½ cup potato starch

⅛ cup sugar

1 tsp. xanthan gum

1 tsp. cider vinegar

½ tsp. salt

¼ cup tapioca starch

1 ½ tbs. corn oil

⅔ cup warm water, plus 1 tbs.

¼ cup corn flour

½ cup cornstarch

Proof yeast in warm water with a pinch of sugar. Combine dry ingredients. Add eggs, oil, vinegar and then proofed yeast. Beat on high speed for 3 minutes. Dough will be sticky and wet, more like cookie dough. Turn out onto board dusted lightly with potato starch. Coat dough just enough so it doesn't stick to hands. Do not knead or add too much starch that will make dough too heavy to rise: the moister the better. Line cookie pan or pizza pan with parchment paper. Gently pat out dough to desired thickness, just barely coating hands as needed. Brush with olive oil. Cover with saran and let rise one hour. Bake at 400 degrees for 15–20 minutes after you add desired toppings. Will just barely brown. Makes 1 large or 4 individual pizzas (kid's size).

Sour Cream Corn Muffins

1 cup corn flour

½ cup sour cream

1 cup cornmeal

⅔ cup sugar

¼ cup corn oil

1 tsp. baking powder

½ cup milk

1 tsp. baking soda

¼ tsp. xanthan gum

1 egg

Mix all ingredients until well incorporated. Pour into greased muffin tins. Bake at 375 degrees for 15–20 minutes until golden. Makes 12 small muffins.

Scones

1 stick of butter	2 ½ cups flour
¼ cup sugar	⅔ cup milk
1 tbs. baking powder	

Optional: add raisins, currents or craisins

Mix all ingredients. Shape into 6 biscuit size balls and flatten. Bake at 350 degrees for about 20 minutes or until golden.

Family Favorite Breaded Chicken

4 chicken breasts	1 cup gluten-free cornflakes
1 egg	(Nature's Path)
½ cup cornmeal	⅓ cup parmesan cheese

Butterfly chicken breasts. Coat in cornmeal. Then dip in an egg wash (beaten egg with 1 tbs. water). Then dip in GF cornflakes mixed with pecorino cheese. Once coated on all sides, refrigerate for at least one hour so crumbs will adhere better. Fry on medium heat in corn oil until golden on all sides . . . about 10–15 minutes total.

Salmon with Creamy Mustard Dill Sauce

4 salmon filets	2 tbs. mustard
1 cup cream	½ tsp. dill
Salt and pepper to taste	

Clean all bones from salmon filet. Broil, sauté or grill filets until moist and cooked through, 10 minutes or so. (In oven, 450 degrees for about 10 minutes, cook in Pyrex, not on aluminum). Prepare sauce in shallow pan. Pour cream into pan; add salt and pepper to taste, mustard and dill. Bring to a boil. Reduce heat and simmer for about 5 minutes until sauce is nice and thick and rich looking. If it gets too thick, add a touch more cream to thin out. Taste to determine if you need salt and pepper. Pour over fish and serve with rice, risotto, broccoli, salad, etc.

Tomato Sauce

1 med. onion, chopped	3 cloves garlic, chopped fine
1 red pepper, chopped	8–10 mushrooms, sliced
1 can crushed tomatoes	1 can tomato paste
1 tsp. sugar	1 tsp baking soda
Salt and pepper to taste	1 tsp. basil

Sauté onion, garlic, mushrooms and peppers in olive oil until tender and golden . . . about 5–7 minutes. Add crushed tomatoes, paste and 2 cans of paste filled with water. Bring to a boil, then immediately reduce heat. Add baking soda; sauce will bubble as acidity from tomatoes comes out from baking soda. Stir until dissolved, then add sugar to sweeten the sauce after bitterness of baking soda. Add basil and salt and pepper to taste. Cook on low heat at a simmer for 1–2 hours. You may add other herbs as desired, like oregano. Pour over favorite pasta! (Tinkyada brown rice is our favorite.)

Meatballs

2 slices GF sandwich bread	1 lb. chopped meat
¼ cup parmesan cheese	1 tsp. parsley
1 egg	Salt and pepper to taste

Toast sandwich bread to dry out. Then soak bread in water. Squeeze and drain bread to get out excess water. Place chopped meat in a bowl. Add bread, egg, cheese, parsley, salt and pepper. Mix well with hands until all incorporated. Take handfuls of meat mix and shape into meatballs of desired size; I usually make 4 inch hamburger size patties. Fry in corn oil until brown on both sides, but not cooked through . . . about 3 minutes a side on medium high heat. Add to tomato sauce and let simmer in sauce for 1–2 hours to continue cooking. This will flavor sauce as well. Meatballs are super tender. You may also choose to add Italian Sweet sausage as well . . . brown on all sides like meatballs, but don't cook through as it will continue cooking in sauce as well.

Featherlight Flour Mix (from Bette Haagman)

1 part cornstarch
1 part rice flour
1 part tapioca starch
1 part potato starch
Makes lighter baked goods.

Nearly Normal Gluten-Free Mix

Can use for 1 cup flour in almost any recipe:

1 cup white rice flour

1 cup potato starch

1 cup cornstarch

½ cup corn flour

½ cup tapioca flour

4 tsp. xanthan gum

Mix and keep in a container and use in baked goods. I tend to cut the xanthan gum by at least 1 tsp., as we like things less gummy!

Olive Focaccia

1 package gluten-free pantry sandwich bread mix

½ cup chopped olives

1 tbs. fresh herbs

Olive oil

Mix bread mix according to package. Add olives and herbs. Grease individual tart pans. Divide mix among 8 pans. Cover and let rise 1 hour or more. Once risen, poke holes in dough with fingertips. Brush olive oil on top and sprinkle with pecorino cheese. Bake at 375 degrees for 20–25 minutes; watch to not over-bake. Cool and then freeze. Can freeze whole or cut into quarters.

Gluten-Free Crepes

2 eggs	1 cup milk
½ tsp. salt	1 tbs. melted butter
¾ cup nearly normal gluten-free mix	

Combine all ingredients in food processor and process until smooth. Refrigerate 2 hours. Will be thin batter.

Pour 2–3 tbs. batter into buttered pre-heated pan and tilt to spread batter evenly. Cook and turn to other side. Stack between paper towels. Fill with fruit or ice cream for dessert, or savory items like chicken and broccoli for lunch or dinner.

Bette Haagman's Fast French Bread

Makes 2–3 small loaves or one big one.

¾ cup rice flour	⅔ cup warm water
⅓ cup tapioca starch	1 tbs. yeast
1 tsp. xanthan gum	1 tbs. melted butter
½ tsp. salt	1 egg white
1 tsp. egg replacer	½ tsp. vinegar
¾ tsp. sugar	

Proof yeast in water with 1/2 tsp. sugar. Place all dry ingredients in mixer. Add wet and then proofed yeast. Beat on high speed for 3 minutes. Dump dough out onto board coated with tapioca starch. Lightly coat in starch enough to shape into either small loaves or one large loaf. Place on greased and corn meal dusted cookie tray. Brush with melted butter, slit diagonally with knife and cover with saran. Let rise until doubled in size about 20 minutes. Bake at 400 degrees for 10–15 minutes for small loaves, 20–30 for large loaf. Cool and enjoy!

Appendix F:
Care and Management of Common Injuries

Injury: Plantar Fasciitis (inflammation of the connective tissue that runs the length of the sole of the foot)

Normal anatomy and physiology:
Healthy fascia provides foot support in walking and running.

Recognize it by these symptoms:
- Stabbing or aching pain in arch of foot or heel
- May be worse in the morning, on waking or after intense activity

Etiology as it relates to training that causes, exacerbates or increases risk of this injury:
- Excessive running in shoes with poor cushioning or little support on hard or uneven surfaces (or downhill running)
- Athletes with high arches or flat feet are particularly prone

- Tight Achilles tendon (poor calf stretching habits) increases risk

Prevention/pre-hab:
- Catch it early!
- Insoles, arch support, orthotics
- Ice and deeply massage foot (stand and roll foot using neoprene hand weight)
- Strengthen: towel scrunch under bare foot
- Stretch calf and plantar fascia
- Anti-inflammatories

Injury: Ankle Sprain

Normal anatomy and physiology:
The ankle is a complicated hinge joint with many ligaments supporting it. When it gets stepped on or you step in a hole, it gets stretched and a partial or complete tear of the ligaments (sprain) may result.

Mechanism of injury/recognize it by these symptoms:
- Usually an inversion; roll the ankle to the outside and injure outer (lateral) ligaments
- Sudden twist or blow
- Acute pain and swelling
- Little or no ability to bear weight
- High risk of chronic joint instability if previous sprains

Treatment for acute injury:

Stop activity (rest), ice, elevate. Brace or splint may be recommended. If unable to bear weight and significant swelling and deformity, X-ray needed to rule out fracture.

Etiology as it relates to training that causes, exacerbates or increases risk of this injury:

- Field conditions can increase the chance of ankle injury
- Athletes who have recovered from previously sprained ankles should continue strengthening (see pre-hab below), though ankle brace or taping are helpful to support
- Once ankle has been sprained, it may become chronically unstable, and prophylactic taping or bracing will be required (lace-up braces often uncomfortable)
- Estimated that more than 75% of sprained ankles are re-sprained

Special risk in growing athletes:

- Poor body control and rough play can increase the chances of ankle injuries

Prevention/pre-hab:

- Strengthen with one-footed hops, one-legged squats, heel walking, toe walking
- Strengthen internal and external rotation using resistance bands around foot
- Work on coordination and balance: wobble boards, foam rollers, one-legged hop and (gentle) shove

- Work dynamic balance and proprioception with jumps, hops, skips
- Stretch through full range of motion after training

When to go to the doctor:
- Deformity in joint. Also, point tenderness over the bone suggests fracture.
- If pain is mild, wait a few days to see. Swelling may prevent bending. This doesn't mean it's broken. If pain persists (must know how kid reacts to pain), see doctor.

Injury: Achilles Tendonitis

Normal anatomy and physiology:
Achilles tendon is a strong connective tissue that attaches the forceful calf muscles to the heel bone (calcaneus).

Recognize it by these symptoms:
- Inflammation
- Dull pain close to the heel; may be sharper with stretching
- Limited ankle flexibility

Etiology as it relates to training that causes, exacerbates or increases risk of this injury:
- Tight calf muscles; insufficient stretching
- Overtraining, especially running and jumping
- High heels cause chronically shortened Achilles tendons; more prone to injury

- Poorly cushioned or poor-fitting heel of shoes may rub and aggravate tendon

Special risk in growing athletes:
- Less likely in kids, more in older youth and adults

Prevention/pre-hab:
- Stretch calf muscles and Achilles tendon after all training and play. Be sure stretch is aligned correctly along the length of the tendon.
- Address over-pronation, if present, with arch supports (orthotics may be necessary)
- If Achilles symptoms are present, ice
- Anti-inflammatories to decrease swelling
- Athlete should stop all running until he can perform heel raises without pain

Injury: Shin Splints

Normal anatomy and physiology:
There are two lower leg bones: the tibia (largest and most prominent) and the fibula, and muscles that run along their length in the front of the shin that dorsi-flex at the ankle and extend the toes. When the tendons of those muscles are strained, small tears in the attachment of muscle to bone become inflamed.

Recognize it by these symptoms:
- Tenderness along crest of shin bone (anterior) or distal 1/3 of tibia (medial or posterior)

- Often a longer, diffuse area of pain
- Pain with applied pressure
- Pain may go away after warm-up
- A short, more narrow area of pain, may be a stress fracture
- In stress fracture: may feel a bump or ridge at site of pain

Etiology as it relates to training that causes, exacerbates or increases risk of this injury:

- Running on hard surfaces in non-cushioned, unsupportive shoes
- Improper running form (e.g., running on the toes or with heavy footfalls)
- Poor calf flexibility and tight tibial muscles which decrease cushioning in landings
- Change in running surface and/or sudden increase in training volume increase risk

Special risk in growing athletes:

- Training volume is of particular concern with active kids
- Multiple teams may mean that no single coach is aware of demands

Prevention/pre-hab:

- Strengthen anterior tibial muscles (toe raises off step)
- Stretch Achilles tendon/calf muscles (lower heel off step)
- Discourage wearing of high heeled shoes
- Arch supports (to decrease pronation) may help
- At first sign of shin splints, reduce training and avoid running on hard surfaces

- Cross friction massage and foam rolling to break up adhesions and promote healing
- Ice for 15 minutes 3x/day

**If shin is tender to direct pressure and there is no relief from pain after resting from training, the athlete should be evaluated for stress fracture using X-ray, likely a bone scan. If an athlete continues to play on a stress fracture, he risks a complete or more involved fracture. An athlete with a stress fracture must rest the leg completely for at least 6 weeks until the bone scan is clear and the athlete is pain free. This is why prevention is imperative! Stress rest!

Injury: Chronic Compartment Syndrome

Normal anatomy and physiology:
Developing muscle tissue is confined in anatomical compartments by inelastic connective tissue surrounding them called fascia. Intense muscle activity can cause fluid and pressure to build up inside the compartment, resulting in pain. Compartment syndrome is sometimes mistaken for shin splints.

Recognize it by these symptoms:
Tightness, pressure or numbness in the lower leg that resolves 30 minutes after stopping activity.

When to go to the doctor:
If pain becomes chronic, especially when tested under training conditions, consult a medical doctor. Surgical compartment release may be advised.

Injury: Osgood Schlatter Disease

Normal anatomy and physiology:
Patellar tendon attaches below the knee joint at the prominent tibial tubercle.

Recognize it by these symptoms:
- Inflammation of the patellar tendon and soft tissue where it attaches to the tibia
- Pain localized to tibial tubercle; may feel a prominent bony bump just below the knee; usually worsens with activity and is relieved with rest
- Site is painful during any activity that bends or extends the knee, especially jumping

Etiology as it relates to training that causes, exacerbates or increases risk of this injury:
- May be present in any kid going through growth spurt but becomes "disease" in young athletes because of constant use of quadriceps muscle pulling on patellar attachment
- Exacerbated by jumping activity; especially common in girls who do ballet
- Commonly grouped as a "growing pain"; it is pain associated with growing tissues but is the overly demanding use (excessive running, jumping, bending), while growing, that results in injury

Special risk in growing athletes:
- Usually emerges during rapid growth (ages 9–13); fast-growing bone is particularly susceptible
- Sever's Disease (calcaneal apophysitis) is a similar "rapid growth" injury to the growth plate of the heel bone; repetitive stress in a susceptible weakened area of growth

Prevention/pre-hab:
- Rest is best: one month off, then re-enter gradually. If rested, will heal in 6–18 months.
- If not total rest, limit activity and competition, taking 2–3 months completely off.
- While knee heals, ice and ibuprofen. If pain persists, see medical doctor.
- After pain subsides, slowly return to activity. Stretch and strengthen with a gentle and gradual progression.
- Generally resolves when kid stops fast growth period (mid-teens)

Injury: Patellofemoral Pain Syndrome/Runner's Knee/ Chondromalacia

Normal anatomy and physiology:
Rounded bone inside the femoral tendon, slides across the joint as the knee bends; when healthy, tracks smoothly in the femoral groove and provides leverage for quadriceps extension of the knee.

Recognize it by these symptoms:
- Pain under the inside or outside edge of knee cap
- Hurts at beginning of activity, then recedes during warm up
- May be especially painful climbing down stairs
- Stiff with prolonged sitting

Etiology as it relates to training that causes, exacerbates or increases risk of this injury:
- Overtraining: excessive # quad extensions causes overuse/repetitive motion injury
- Overpronation adds to misaligning pull on quad tendon
- Continuously poor tracking with high intensity use can cause permanent arthritic damage under the kneecap, known as chondromalacia, which wears away the articular cartilage under the kneecap (it doesn't regenerate)

Special risk in growing athletes:
- Special concern in female athletes, increased "Q" angle (angle between femur and line of quad pull) with wider hips can tend to stress/torque tendon out of alignment
- Tight IT band also contributes to misalignment, particularly in females

Prevention/pre-hab:
- Reduce running; run on softer surface
- Insoles, inserts or orthotics may help

- Strengthen quads, especially VMO (most medial quad muscle) to create better patellar tracking (conservative strengthening: straight leg raises; add ankle weights to increase intensity); AVOID putting weight on knee in bent position
- Stretch hamstrings and calves to decrease pronation
- Stretch IT band; use of foam roller is recommended
- A brace with a patellar cutout may be prescribed, or taping to correct poor patellar tracking can be done preventively and provide instant relief.

Injury: ACL Tear or Rupture

Normal anatomy and physiology:
Anterior cruciate ligament crosses knee joint from anterior tibia to posterior femur, assisting in stabilizing and preventing excessive rotation in the knee, preventing tibia from moving too far forward relative to the femur; ACL works as an agonist/synergist with the hamstring and antagonistically to the quadriceps.

Recognize it by these symptoms:
- Instability in the knee with swelling, usually within 24 hours; reported as unpredictable or giving way
- May hear a tear or pop in the knee on injury
- Usually significant pain; occasionally no pain

Etiology as it relates to training that causes, exacerbates or increases risk of this injury:

- Particularly concerning because injury is frequently non-contact, a "plant and give way" phenomenon. Fitness level is not necessarily a predictor, although "exposures"—or numbers of practices, scrimmages and games—correlate with injuries.

- Torn ACLs generally require surgical repair for athletes. Rehab and recovery time is six months to one year, with many recommending increasing this time to return to play to decrease re-tearing the repair and/or putting the other knee at risk. Recovery from surgery also dependent on type of graft used. (Autograft: using "own" tissue; requires recovery of this harvest before rehab can begin. Allograft: cadaver tissue; no delay in rehab. Autograft has shown a much lower risk of re-tear in young athletes.)

Special risk in growing athletes:

- Females in the 15–25 age range who participate in cutting and turning sports are particularly at risk, although ACL tears are happening in increasingly younger athletes. Some have reported that males are at similar risk, but the injury strikes later, usually in their 20s and 30s.

- Imbalances in relative quad/hamstring strength and range of motion increase risk.

- Female patterned movement also appears to play a role. More straight-legged stopping and cutting, as well as bending from the waist rather than the knees to change direction, are typical. Anatomical imbalances and habitual movement patterns coupled with changes in coordination put girls who are first developing mature anatomy and strength at particular risk.

Prevention/pre-hab:
Dynamic warm-up and injury prevention training to include:
- Agility, balance, proprioceptive training
- Hamstring strengthening to decrease quadriceps' dominant strength and L/R imbalances
- Outer thigh/hip: dynamic strengthening to resist knee valgus (bending inward)
- Adjust movement patterns to favor bent knee (hinge) landing and change of direction (activate hamstrings)
- Teach/train use of multi-step stopping techniques
- Neuromuscular/footwork training starting at earliest ages of play to develop quick motor recruitment

Injury: Torn Meniscus

Normal anatomy and physiology:
Dual cartilage discs in the knee joint providing cushioning between tibia and femur and additional "fit," which lends stability to joint

Recognize it by these symptoms (dependent on the severity of the tear):
- Pain upon straightening the knee and with cutting and rotation
- Clicking or locking in the knee

- Pain surrounding medial or lateral joint line
- Swelling is usually acute, but may be delayed, intermittent or persistent

Etiology as it relates to training that causes, exacerbates or increases risk of this injury:

- Usually occurs when the foot is planted, bearing body weight, and the upper body twists/rotates

Treatment options depend on location and severity of the tear:

- Peripheral injury, nearer capsular blood flow, has better chance of healing
- Minor tear may heal on its own but needs to be rested
- Extensive tear usually requires surgery. Location of the tear determines whether it can be repaired; if it is toward the outside of the joint near a blood supply, repair has a better chance of success. May be repaired by re-anchoring torn portion or meniscectomy, where part or all of the tear is removed.
- Surgical repair requires, at minimum, 3-6 months recovery: 4-6 weeks limited motion and bracing to walk without bending to protect repair; 6 weeks of basic physical therapy and rehab, then 3 months of active rehab and recovery PT.
- Athletes usually may return to play after repair once they have full range of motion, no swelling and good strength. They MUST follow a protocol of gradual

increase in balanced muscle strengthening under the care of a physical therapist or qualified exercise physiologist or trainer.

Special risk in growing athletes:

- Younger athletes are more likely to have a peripheral injury. Their menisci are healthier, and there is more fluid in the joint supporting the menisci.
- Aging makes menisci more brittle, more "white," with no blood supply and offering less cushioning. Older menisci are more likely to tear and require excision rather than repair.

Prevention/pre-hab:

- Teach and train athletes to execute movements using bent knee mechanics
- Agility training to elude blows to knee and/or to "fold" to hurdle tackles
- Bracing may be recommended to control side-to-side motion in at-risk knee

Injury: Iliotibial (IT) Band Syndrome

Normal anatomy and physiology:

The IT band is a strong strand of connective tissue that runs along the outside of the thigh from the knee to the pelvis. When healthy, it helps stabilize the knee and hip. In knee flexion and extension it may rub against the lateral tubercle of the tibia, where the iliotibial tract inserts.

Recognize it by these symptoms:
- Pain or ache on the outside of the knee or the lateral hip at the iliac crest
- Pain during activity that may recede after
- Swelling may be absent if motion is normal

Etiology as it relates to training that causes, exacerbates or increases risk of this injury:
- When the IT band is too tight, subject to overuse or is inflamed or weak (or synergistic muscles/hip abductors or rotators are weak), use and especially overuse/high intensity training and the accompanying friction result in inflammation and pain.

Special risk in growing athletes:
- Growth spurts lengthen bones, which increases tension on elastic tissues like the IT band.

Prevention/pre-hab:
- Stretch: lying, flex one leg to hip level and drop to side, keep as straight as possible
- Stretch: stand arm's length away from wall with palm resting flat on wall; cross leg nearest the wall behind other foot and position flat on floor; lean into wall
- Stretch: feet same as above but bow and bend to side
- Stretch: use foam roller on affected area
- Strengthen synergistic muscles: outside hip gluteus medius (side leg raises, doggies, hip hikes standing on step or box)

- Strengthen medial quadriceps (VMO = vastus medialis obliquus)
- Core strengthening exercises are important to support torso and lessen hip "give" to the side on landing in upright movement
- Additional stretch: hip flexors and quads to maintain healthy hip alignment

Injury: Groin Pull or Strain

Normal anatomy and physiology:
Muscles in the groin (inner thigh) area are adductor muscles that adduct the thigh (pull legs together) and assist in rotating the thigh at the hip and in flexing at the hip.

Mechanism of injury:
- Sudden forceful stress on the groin area muscles, which overstretches or tears muscle fibers. May hear a popping or feel a snapping at time of injury, followed by severe pain

Recognize it by these symptoms:
- Pain and tenderness in the groin and the inside of the thigh
- Pain with hip adduction, bringing the legs together
- Pain with hip flexion to raise the knee

Treatment:
Rest, ice to reduce pain and swelling, thigh compression using an elastic ace bandage or taping

Etiology as it relates to training that causes, exacerbates or increases risk of this injury:
- Groin/adductor muscles are generally much weaker than hip flexor muscles; they assist the strong, active quadriceps group. They are prime movers in hip flexion while externally rotated, used for example to send a ball with the instep or inner foot surface. Overuse or overreaching effort in this motion without proper warm-up, stretching and strengthening results in strains.

Special risk in growing athletes:
Developing, but imbalanced, strength and new limb growth make young athletes particularly prone to groin pull. Particularly common in boys, mid growth spurt.

Prevention/pre-hab:
- Strengthen the adductor muscles, pelvic stabilizing muscles and core muscles during pre-season
- Warm up hip motion in the diagonal planes (stand with hand support on wall or teammate and swing leg inward and outward with rotation) before all practices and games
- Stretch the inner thigh after practices and games
- Take extra care to stretch gradually and strengthen if an athlete has had previous groin pulls

- Be sure groin is fully healed before testing it with effort. Re-injury is common and can be harder to treat and take longer to heal.

Injury: Muscle Cramps

Normal anatomy and physiology:
Sudden, extreme, involuntary, sustained contraction of a muscle.

Recognize it by these symptoms:
- Muscle spasm
- Pain
- Temporary near paralysis

Etiology as it relates to training that causes, exacerbates or increases risk of this injury:
- Dehydration, electrolyte depletion and fatigue with long, hot training
- Special concern in hot months
- Heavy equipment/gear can add to load on fluid balance system

Special risk in growing athletes:
- Insufficient rest in young athletes may make them more susceptible.

Prevention/pre-hab:
- Teach proper hydrating techniques
- Stretch after training and play

- Allow sufficient rest and recovery
- Take sufficient drink breaks
- If longer than 60-minute training, encourage electrolyte replacement

Injury: Side Stitch

Normal anatomy and physiology:
Intake of a deep breath is assisted by the diaphragm, a muscle that extends across the bottom of the rib cage. Insufficient oxygen supply to the working diaphragm muscle, especially at initiation of exercise, may be the cause of side stitch.

Recognize it by these symptoms:
- Stabbing pain under the lower edge of the rib cage; usually occurs at the beginning of exercise

Etiology as it relates to training that causes, exacerbates or increases risk of this injury:
- Improper warm-up and low fitness contribute to side stitch
- If stitch occurs, stop and stretch holding arm up and lean to side away from cramp. If athlete cannot stop, slow the pace and breathe deeply and regularly through pursed lips (should be able to hear breath on exhale).

Special risk in growing athletes:
- Tendency for young athletes to "jump in" to action may bring on side stitch. Establish protocol for warm-up.

- Tight schedules (eat and run) also invite side stitch. Be aware of scheduling and nutritional needs.

Prevention/pre-hab:
- Warm athletes up gradually and properly
- Be sure substitutes warm up again before entering game
- Establish sufficient fitness levels for game demands
- Caution athletes about eating food that is hard to digest right before training/play. (See nutrition section for healthy eating for performance.)

Injury: Concussion

A concussion is a mild traumatic brain injury that occurs as the result of a blow to the head or body with force transmitted to the head, accelerates the brain inside the skull (whiplash-like) and temporarily impairs brain function. Severe or repeated trauma can result in prolonged symptoms and deficits.

Normal anatomy and physiology:

The brain sits atop the "brain stem" at the top of the spinal column and is bathed in cerebrospinal fluid and protected by several membranes and the bony skull. Sudden traumatic force can shake the brain on its stem, resulting in whiplash-like damage to neural tissue.

Recognize it by these symptoms:
- Headache
- Dizziness and/or nausea

- Impaired balance
- Blurred vision and/or light sensitivity
- Dazed or stunned affect
- Confusion or mental fogginess
- Impaired memory (e.g., they answer questions slowly or repeat questions)
- Headaches that worsen
- Seizures
- Neck pain
- Marked drowsiness
- Repeated vomiting
- Slurred speech
- Increased confusion and/or inability to recognize people or places
- Weakness or numbness in the arms or legs
- Unusual behavior change, including increased irritability
- Loss of consciousness

Etiology as it relates to training that causes, exacerbates or increases risk of this injury:

- Training young athletes to use proper heading technique is essential with gradual exposure to the basic skill and building to full execution
- Repeated heading can be dangerous (brain injury may be cumulative)
- Athletes who show any symptoms should be removed from play until asymptomatic

Special risk in growing athletes:
- The growing brain is particularly susceptible to brain injury (teens at special risk with young brains and new heading skills)
- Female athletes at higher risk, possibly because of weaker backs, torsos and necks, and different heading technique

Prevention/pre-hab:
- Strengthen back, neck and torso, especially in female athletes
- Teach heading technique using entire upper torso, not just head and neck
- Gradually introduce the skill with little or no head contact
- Establish skill before adding weighted ball and game environment
- Teach and coach skill rather than force

Appendix G:

Communicating with a Health Care Professional

If you do have to go see your doctor, go prepared to answer these questions:

1. Describe the onset of your symptoms. The history of your injury (what happened when you were injured) if it was acute and you know the moment you hurt it. If it has been ongoing, how long ago did it start?

2. Pinpoint the pain and be able to identify what makes it worse or makes it better. Have you attempted treatment of any sort?

3. How has the injury progressed? Has it changed, gotten worse? Gotten better? Does it feel different now than when you first became aware of it?

4. Have you changed anything in your training or play? New surface? New team? New shoes? Increased training time?

5. What else hurts? Bring your "injury history," a list of past injuries and how you've treated them.

6. Bring your training shoes. The kind of equipment you use and the wear patterns on it may provide clues to diagnosis.

Appendix H:
First Aid and How to Pack Your Med Kit

Basic First Aid

RICE is the acronym for the recommended treatment of acute injuries such as sprains, strains, bruises and contusions (Rest, Ice, Compression, Elevation).

Begin RICEing the injury immediately. Instruct athletes to continue icing at home: 20 minutes on and 20 minutes off, three consecutive times. Avoid prolonged direct contact of ice with skin by placing a thin layer of paper towel or wrap between.

- Icing the injured area causes the blood vessels to constrict, limiting swelling and easing pain.
- Compression with an elastic bandage helps reduce swelling, decreases jostling and supports the injured site, which reduces pain, especially when the athlete must be moved.
- Resting and elevating the injured area decreases fluid accumulation and helps control pain.

Stocking Your First Aid Kit

- Assorted adhesive bandages
- Elastic wrap/ace wrap
- Gauze pads
- Latex gloves
- 2 instant ice packs
- Antibiotic ointment cream/Neosporin
- Alcohol prep pads
- Antiseptic pads
- Gauze roll
- Tape roll
- Scissors
- Mole skin pads
- Bag of hair ties
- **List of team emergency contact numbers
- **Bug spray

Attending a Red Cross First Aid certification course is recommended for all coaches.

Resources

Resources for Chapter 4:

Fitting Fitness into the Practice Plan

- Best Practices for Coaches (http://www.vysa.com/docs/coaches/Best_Practices.pdf) is a terrific resource for coaching youth soccer from the Virginia Youth Soccer Association, with a comprehensive outline for all ages, stages and abilities.
- Games Kids Play: http://www.gameskidsplay.net

Fit2Finish video resources

- Crazy days warm-up: https://www.youtube.com/watch?v=o42FawclTEc
- Crazy days in the zoo: https://www.youtube.com/watch?v=59SjtO3gA9Q
- Obstacle course: https://www.youtube.com/watch?v=tf678sxNFwo
- Shove the gamut: https://www.youtube.com/watch?v=WLc6Fy_lUOE
- Basic agility course: https://www.youtube.com/watch?v=NLo6eY081ys
- Expanded agility course: https://www.youtube.com/watch?v=y6uSW1suid0

- Leap and hold: https://www.youtube.com/
  watch?v=FCT5u-3hPAg
- Partner 2-legged pushes: https://www.youtube.com/
  watch?v=Jpa4kLJsOX4
- Resistance band tag: https://www.youtube.com/
  watch?v=5kFruwvPPz8
- Hop and volley: https://www.youtube.com/
  watch?v=zed9GXhQDvo
- V-passing: https://www.youtube.com/
  watch?v=K0o8eqFtIgc
- Fit2Finish dynamic warm-up: https://www.youtube.
  com/watch?v=Fu5MiL1XHN8

Resources for Chapter 5:
Flexibility, Stretching and Recovery

- Active Isolated Stretching: http://www.stretchingusa.
  com/active-isolated-stretching
- FIFA 11+ program's strength and balance builders
  by Alex Morgan and Cobi Jones: http://www.
  youtube.com/playlist?list=PL-W9Gn-XDQ_
  pIeE4mo1mgBb4OwyGc0UGU
- Basic stretching routine for soccer coaches and athletes:
  http://fit2finish.com/soccer-stretches-for-coaches-and-
  athletes/
- Sample stretching program that uses the rope: http://
  fit2finish.com/stretches-for-athletes-who-run/
- To learn more about using recovery as a training tool:
  http://fit2finish.com/work-and-recovery-are-essential-
  to-high-performanceinterval-training-is-most-gamelike/

- To find out how much soccer is too much to be healthy for your kid: http://fit2finish.com/everybody-wants-a-piece-of-my-kid-calculate-dont-negotiate/

Resources for Chapter 6:
Fueling the Athlete for Performance

General nutrition
- Nancy Clark, MS, RD, *Nancy Clark's Sports Nutrition Guidebook: Eating to Fuel Your Active Lifestyle* (Leisure Press, 1990)
- http://nutritiondata.self.com/topics/glycemic-index: Site offers comprehensive nutrition information and analysis, and indicates digestibility of common foods
- http://glycemicindex.com/: interactive glycemic index

Eating disorders
- National Eating Disorder Association (NEDA): http://www.nationaleatingdisorders.org/
- Renfrew Center (http://renfrewcenter.com/): eating disorder information and literature
- 10 tips for coaches: http://renfrewcenter.com/sites/default/files/Ten_Things_Coaches_%26_Trainers_Can_Do_0.pdf
- *Surviving an Eating Disorder: Strategies for Family and Friends*, by Michele Siegel, PhD; Judith Brisman, PhD; and Margot Weinshel, MSW

- *Life Without ED: How One Woman Declared Independence from Her Eating Disorder and How You Can Too*, by Jenni Schaefer and Thom Rutledge
- *Dying to Be Thin: Understanding and Defeating Anorexia Nervosa and Bulimia*, by Ira Sacker, MD, and Marc A. Zimmer, PhD

Celiac disease

- Celiac Sprue Association (http://www.csaceliacs.org/): Best website for updates on information. You can order the product guide from them for $20. A new one comes out every October.
- Celiac Disease Foundation: http://www.celiac.org/
- Camp Celiac: http://campceliac.org/
- Cookbooks:
- Bette Haagman: *The Gluten-Free Gourmet*
- Jules Shepard: *Nearly Normal Cooking for Gluten-Free Eating*
- Rebecca Reilly: *Gluten-Free Baking* (she was a former pastry chef)
- *Living Without* magazine (http://livingwithout.com): We love this magazine, and it provides great recipes and information. Comes out quarterly. We really enjoy getting this— worth investing in!

Resources for Chapter 7:
Beating Injuries to Keep Your Athletes in the Game

- Red Cross Sports Training Safety courses for coaches: http://www.redcross.org/take-a-class

- To learn more about strengthening players against concussions: http://fit2finish.com/strengthening-our-girls-against-concussions-three-simple-ways-to-build-neck-and-core-strength-while-keeping-it-fun/
- For helpful information, links, handouts and an online training course on concussions: http://www.cdc.gov/concussion/HeadsUp/youth.html

Reading list addressing "changing the culture of youth sports"

Jim Thompson, *Positive Coaching, Building Character and Self-Esteem through Sports* (Warde Publishers, 1995).

Shane Murphy, *The Cheers and the Tears* (Jossey-Bass, 1999).

Bob Bigelow, Tom Moroney and Linda Hall, *Just Let the Kids Play* (Health Communications, Inc., 2001).

Tony DiCicco and Colleen Hacker, *Catch Them Being Good,* (Penguin, 2002).

Harry Sheehy with Danny Peary, *Raising a Team Player* (Storey Publishing, 2002).

George Selleck, *Raising a Good Sport in an In-Your-Face World* (Contemporary Books, 2003).

Dr. Joel Fish with Susan Magee, *101 Ways to be a Terrific Sports Parent* (Fireside, 2003).

Jim Thompson, *The Double-Goal Coach* (HarperCollins, 2003). Thompson expands on his ideas from *Positive Coaching*, above.

John Wooden and Jay Carty, *Coach Wooden's Pyramid of Success* (Regal Books, 2005).

Michael Sokolove, *Warrior Girls* (Simon & Schuster, 2008).

Jeffrey Rhoads, *The Joy of Youth Sports: Creating the Best Youth Sports Experience for Your Child* (Avaplay Press, 2009).

John O'Sullivan, *Changing the Game* (Morgan James Publishing, 2014).

Glossary

Adenosine triphosphate (ATP)—high-energy molecule in the cell which stores energy in phosphate bonds; sometimes called the "powerhouse of the cell"

Aerobic—using, requiring, or in the presence of oxygen

- Aerobic metabolism—complete breakdown of organic substrates into carbon dioxide and water, yielding much energy as ATP (requires oxygen and mitochondria)
- Aerobic zone—training zone where oxygen supplies are sufficient to meet demands for energy production

Anaerobic—in the absence of oxygen

- Anaerobic glycolysis—breakdown of glucose to lactate (does not require oxygen) yielding energy for first 2 minutes of exercise
- Anaerobic threshold/lactate threshold—point at which lactic acid produced in the muscles begins to accumulate

in the blood; defines the upper limit of work that can be sustained aerobically

Anterior cruciate ligament (ACL)—one of 2 criss-crossing ligaments in the knee joint which acts to resist anterior translation and medial rotation of the tibia relative to the femur

Articulation—synonym for joint, or the relative association between bones at a joint (ie. the femur and the tibia *articulate* at the knee joint)

Ballistic stretching—stretching that involves a bouncing motion which forces the joint into an extended range of motion

Bone remodeling—reshaping of bone structure according to forces which push and pull

Cartilage—firm, elastic connective tissue with gelatinous matrix and an abundance of fibers (3 types are hyaline, fibrous, elastic)

Circuit training—system of training which employs stations or a variety of exercises through which one moves, often done as a group activity for exposure to multiple, varied training demands

Contraction of muscle

- Concentric contraction—a type of muscle contraction in which muscles shorten while generating force
- Eccentric/lengthening contraction—muscle elongates while generating force which is insufficient to overcome an opposing force

- Isometric contraction—muscle generates force against an equal load, resulting in no muscle shortening or movement
- Isotonic contraction—muscular force overcomes resistance of load and shortens, resulting in movement

Concussion—mild traumatic brain injury which results from collision or impact

Connective tissue—group of body tissues which connect, support or surround other tissues or organs (ligaments, tendons, cartilage are examples)

Core strength—muscles underlying the torso which are points of fixation and support for movement

CP (creatine phosphate)—energy-rich molecule inside the cell which supplements ATP

Cross training—pattern of alternating training demands to offer work and recovery to muscle groups and energy systems

Disordered eating—eating patterns which are ineffective in supplying proper nutrients for health and activity (extreme calorie restriction or extreme dieting may be early signs of developing eating disorders)

Eating disorders—severe disturbances in eating habits, most prominently anorexia nervosa and bulimia, which often require medical intervention

Dynamic stretching—smooth, patterned movement designed to move the body through full range of motion at one or multiple joints

Dynamic warm-up—fitness routine which employs dynamic stretching and movement, progressing in intensity to prepare the body for activity or performance

Female athlete triad—a syndrome where disordered eating, ammenorhea, and decreased bone density are present and result in significant increased risk for stress fracture. (Often seen in athletes participating in sports which emphasize leanness or low body weight.)

Flexibility—range of motion through which the limbs or body parts are able to move

Glycogen—storage form of glucose (found primarily in muscle and liver)

Growth plate/epiphyseal plate—the area of growing tissue near the ends of the long bones in children and adolescents which determines the future length of the mature bone (the weakest areas of the growing skeleton, thus especially vulnerable to injury)

Interval training—an efficient method of training which employs alternating work and rest intervals of a prescribed length and intensity to maximize training of specific energy systems

Lactic acid/lactate—compound produced from anaerobic glycolysis which increases if oxygen demand is greater than supply (burning sensation attributed to its accumulation in muscle tissue)

Ligament—tough fibrous, inelastic, connective tissue which connects bone to bone, providing support and stability at a joint

Meniscus—specialized, crescent-shaped cushion of cartilage in the knee joint

Motor neurons—nerve fibers which conduct electrical impulses to the muscles

Muscle group members
- Prime mover—the muscle supplying the greatest force in the movement
- Agonists and/or synergists—muscles contributing additional force with the prime mover
- Antagonists—muscles whose contraction opposes the force generated by the prime mover; their gradual eccentric contraction controls the speed of motion in progress
- Stabilizers—muscles providing support by contracting to prevent unwanted movement or to hold the non-moving parts in place

Muscle memory—pattern of stimulus and response which occurs after much rehearsal of exact motor mechanics

Overload principle—for training to occur, the demand on muscle or body system must be greater than its typical load

Overtraining—training without sufficient rest and recovery which causes chronic breakdown of tissues and often results in injury

Perceived exertion—level of effort perceived by the athlete; relates to training demand but influenced by mental, emotional and physical condition of the athlete

Periodization—systematic planning of physical training involving progressive cycling of various demands over time, intending to reach peak performance for important competitions

Plyometric training (also called **jump training**)—uses repetitions of quick and explosive movements to increase speed and power

Proprioception—position sensation offered by specialized receptors in muscles or joints

Reflex (muscle)—rapid stimulus-response of a nerve/muscle pairing which occurs automatically

Resting heart rate—pulse at rest, best measured before rising in the morning

SAID (Specific Adaptations to Imposed Demands) principle—training design which matches physical demands to body response and recovery for gradual improvement in fitness and performance

Sensory neurons—nerve fibers which conduct electrical impulses from body sensors to the central nervous system and brain

Specificity of training—a guiding principle of training which states that the physical improvement expected is specific to the kind of training, speed of training, and body part or energy system trained

Sprain—an injury to one or more ligaments

Static stretching—lengthening of muscles by holding the body in an extended position

Strain—an injury to a muscle or a tendon

Stress fracture—a bone fracture resulting from high intensity and/or repetitive force which subjects the bone to continuous stress

Stretch reflex—rapid, automatic muscle contraction in response to a quick stretch

Target heart rate—heart rate level for a desired training effect (usually expressed as a range)

Tendon—tough, fibrous, connective tissue which connects muscle to bone and can withstand great tension

Training intensity—the load or demand to which a body is subjected, applied in a measured quantity (e.g., lbs, distance, speed), its effect measured as a percent of heart rate response or ventilatory capacity